GOLF
FOR WEEKEND WARRIORS

GOLF
FOR WEEKEND WARRIORS

A GUIDE TO EVERYTHING FROM BUNKERS TO BIRDIES TO BACK SPASMS

RANDY HOWE

THE LYONS PRESS
Guilford, Connecticut
An imprint of The Globe Pequot Press

The Lyons Press is an imprint of The Globe Pequot Press.

10 9 8 7 6 5 4 3 2 1

Printed in the United States of America

Designed by Maggie Peterson

Library of Congress Cataloging-in-Publication Data

Howe, Randy.
  Golf for weekend warriors : a guide to everything from back spasms to
bunkers to birdies / Randy Howe.
      p. cm.
  ISBN 1-59228-608-9 (trade paper)
  1. Golf--Miscellanea. I. Title.

GV967.H65 2005
796.352--dc22

2005006057

To Bill and Brian Murray. Danke Schoen

Acknowledgments

A debt of gratitude to…
Ann, for being such a good sport. One of these days,
you and me and the Par Three at Guilford Links.
You're gonna love this game!
Willie, for lending me the latest in AV technology.
Andrew, Craig, Dave, Greg, James, Jeremy, John, Marc, Mike,
Tim, and Tim, for being such super supermodels.
And finally Alicia, for not only tolerating my athletic
infatuations but encouraging them.

Disclaimer

Have you seen my ball?

Table of Contents

Hacker Facts:
From *Webster's Old School Dictionary*

game (gãm) *noun* **1** any form of play or way of playing; amusement; recreation; sport; frolic **2** any specific contest, engagement, self-injurious behavior involving a score, other players, beer, trash talk, sweat, mind-over-matter, stakes **3** a way or quality of playing in competition **4** any test of skill, courage, or endurance **5** wild animals that are hunted and killed because they are a detriment to the golf course

Introduction:
If, Only If

I was thirteen that Christmas. Old enough to want to be treated like a man, but young enough to still want toys. When my parents handed me my first set of golf clubs, both wishes came true. Shiny silver Wilson clubs in a bright red bag: a starter set from Caldor's. I was on my way.

Naturally, I went for the longest, largest club first. Hellooo, driver! "This one ought to be easy to hit," I remember saying. "It's so much bigger than the others." And you know, the first time I hit it, it *was* easy. I brought the club back slowly and I swung somewhat cautiously, not trying to crush the ball. But crush I did. A fortuitous drive straight like arrow and destined for the middle of the fairway. There is no joy like watching a golf ball take its time to pass through the high blue sky. It's a sight to see when somebody else does it, but when you're the propeller, the feeling is like standing at the edge of the Grand Canyon for the first time, except you get to look up and out instead of down, down, down.

Next, I pulled the putter out. It would only be another twenty years before I'd figure out that this is the most important, most-often used club in the bag. For all of us golfers, weekend warriors and professionals alike, the putter is the one club that can lead to golfing glory or doom and gloom—more so than any other. It's simple math. A matter of inches.

One at a time, I proceeded to remove the clubs from the bag, taking half swings and noticing the difference in length between the woods and the wedges; how as the numbers on the irons rose higher, the angle of the club face grew more severe. When I got to my stocking, all of the essential accoutrements were there: tees, a tiny two-pronged fork for repairing the green, a glove, and five sleeves of balls. (As if fifteen balls would ever be enough to get me through a round!) Four months later, I teed off for the first time at Mohansic, a gem of a county course in Yorktown Heights, New York.[1] $12 for a youth to walk. And walk I did. Again and again and again.

I just couldn't stay away. Not from Mohansic and not from any of the other courses I've ravaged over the years, ripping up divots and slicing shots into condominium windows, onto snack bar roofs, through caddyshack windows, and off of trees, rocks, geese, and golf carts. I just couldn't get enough of the game and to this day, I still can't. With the gift of golf, my parents pointed me towards that first fairway and so . . . I blame them!!!

Golf is the sweetest obsession in that when I suffer through the doldrums, it still ain't so bad. A couple of awful holes. A string of bad outings. So what? At least I was out playing. But I'm telling you, if I don't get out to play regularly, I start to go into convulsions. The little muscle below my right eye twitches like a Mexican jumping bean. I speak in tongues and spend hours on my hands and knees, getting as close as possible to the crab grass in my backyard. I become convinced that it's the Bermuda grass of a well-cut fairway or, better yet, the bent grass of a tenderly cared for green. I even tried to get the yard tight as a green once: my wife convinced me to stop biting the grass by making an emergency tee time. Apparently, they were familiar with my condition at the pro shop.

---

[1] *I hit that first drive long and straight and soon thereafter acquired a slice so bad that my boys nicknamed me Sir Slice-A-Lot!*

Admittedly, in the years following that fateful Christmas, I didn't necessarily love golf purely for the sport of it. I enjoyed being able to drive around in a cart, drinking beers and hazing my friends for their awful play, even as I lived up to my Sir Slice-A-Lot name. Teenaged boys are a dangerous commodity, especially when given a motorized vehicle, golf clubs, and a bunch of aimless balls. Even when I went off to college, golf was less like a sport and more like happy hour with a scorecard.

But maturity can only be put off for so long and with a daughter came adulthood. In addition to purchasing life insurance and a Subaru, I started to take lessons. I began to care about my score. And as much as I relished competing against others, I was eager to beat myself. To just shave one or two strokes off of the handicap would be worthy of celebration! Like that sailor kissing the nurse in Times Square, I'd sweep my wife up into my arms. I'd tell her of my new and improved handicap and then we'd kiss for the camera. I'd forget all my golfing frustrations and she'd forget the image of me, face first in the firmament, chewing on crab grass and muttering about my fickle putter. A joyous moment, but still, a little voice in the back of my head, unwilling to let me rest for even a moment. A little voice saying, "If only I could break ninety."

If. . . The phrase that is as responsible for my addiction as any of the beautiful courses, memorable shots, or any of that male bonding hoopla. If . . . It is the mantra of the delusional optimist. The rationalization of a weekend warrior hacker.

If only I could plant my approach shots right next to the pin.
If only I could rely on that putter.
If only I knew how to get out of bunkers.
If only I could drive three hundred yards.
Straight.
Consistently.

If only I could concentrate more.

If only I took those lessons like I'd planned.

If only I left the cooler and cigars at home.

If only I could ignore the urge to try and out-drive my buddies.

If only I could play every day. I would. I really would.[2]

So, for giving me my first set of clubs, I'd like to say thank you, Mom and Dad. Many of my happiest memories came compliments of this great game. Still, I'd be a lot happier if I could break ninety. If only I could say "eighty-nine" as we all tumble into the nineteenth hole.

If . . .

---

[2] *This is called retirement and I just have to come to terms with the fact that mine is still thirty years off. Ugh!*

GOLF
FOR WEEKEND WARRIORS

1

A History of the Game

I used to live next door to a man named Ernie. He was born back when golf clubs had names rather than numbers and although golf existed long before he swung his first brassie, Ernie was my link to the history of the game. He was nostalgia and knowledge all rolled into one, living proof that golf, like America itself, is for everybody.

Even before the shrinkage of old age, I could tell that Ernie had never been physically prolific. He stood at five-foot-eight and weighed no more than 150 pounds in the latter years of his life. In addition to his physique, Ernie was a man who'd gone into business as a butcher rather than go to college. Italian was his first language—certainly not what people envision when they think of golf. But, you know what? Ninety-nine-point-nine percent of golfers are *not* descendants of the Mayflower. Ninety-nine-point-nine percent of golfers do *not*—present company included—

possess an Ivy League degree. This is not, as some would believe, the sport of doctors, lawyers, and CEOs. Ninety-nine-point-nine percent of golfers—as we can almost all attest!—are not millionaires. Golf is a game for regular folks. It's bowling with small balls instead of big, one pin instead of ten. Just compare the shiny shoes: you'll see I'm right.

A stone wall separated my yard from Ernie's and we used to converse from our respective sides. The divide grew smaller as we talked golf, Ernie doing the telling and me doing the listening. We rarely got into family and never into religion or politics, but there was plenty of golf. It was common ground for two guys from two very different generations.

Ernie's gang—twelve golfers known around Mohansic as The Thundering Herd—was legendary for great golf and great tee times. Not only did they always manage to get the first slot on Saturday, Ernie scored four aces over the years. Four holes-in-one. Four nods in *Golf Digest*. Dr. Francis Scheid, a professor of mathematics at Boston University, says that the chances of getting a hole-in-one in any given round are 5,000-to-1. And the man did it four times—all four par 3s at Mohansic. Amazing. Almost as amazing were those tee times. The Thundering Herd would take turns, two guys pulling into the course at 3:00 AM and driving as close to the starter's booth as they could get, a whole line of cars snaking behind them as the sun began to hint at the horizon. Coffee cups, cigarettes, and war stories up front, golf clubs, spikes, and a little nip of something in the back. Old school.

And you know, Ernie told me once that he missed the bonding after Mohansic installed its phone-in tee-time system. I now understand what he meant.

Our time at the stone wall coming to a close, Ernie would rush into the garage and bring me an egg carton full of used balls.

I never used them—most appeared to be older than I was—but I appreciated the gesture. The game begins and ends, after all, with a golf ball. Not necessarily the *same* golf ball, but . . .

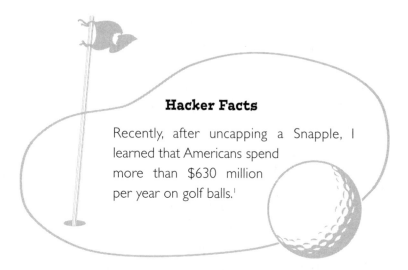

Hacker Facts

Recently, after uncapping a Snapple, I learned that Americans spend more than $630 million per year on golf balls.[1]

It was on January 1, 1932, right around the time Ernie got his version of the Caldor starter set, that a regulation weight and size was established for golf balls by the United States Golf Association (USGA). Following standards set by the British Golf Association, the weight was set at a maximum of 1.62 ounces with a diameter no less than 1.68 inches. Later, after testing apparatus was developed to measure speed, a maximum velocity of 250 feet per second was added. This, to make sure John Daly doesn't kill any of the players in front of him.

Before standardization, golf went through its original R&D phase as some clever fellow decided to boil goose feathers and stuff them into a pouch of leather. This version of the golf ball

---

[1] *I'll admit, I account for like 25 percent of that!*

was called, appropriately enough, a feathery. (I could swear Ernie gave me a feathery once.) Next came the "gutty" or Gutta-Percha ball. This was the name of the Malaysian tree whose sap, when hardened, made for a more reliable, longer-lasting ball. Although geese can fly, and fly straight like arrow, the tree sap made for much happier golfers. Around this time, some golf balls were also made of wood, but the substance was too malleable, even more so than a modern ball after hitting a cart path, condominium, or the head of another player. Then there was the rubber phase, followed by a rhino ball made from the mucus of baby rhinoceroses. (Okay, so I made that last one up.) Rather than experiment with animal snot, scientists got busy on the ball we all know and love/hate today, pushing dimples into the hard rubber surface so as to aid in distance and accuracy. I'm still waiting, though, for someone to develop the "Honer." What I envision is a ball that could tie into the cart's Global Positioning System (GPS). Finally, finally I could stop losing so many balls.

If you put Ernie and me together, we were 150 percent Italian. And so it's only natural that we credited the game of golf to the Romans rather than the Dutch or the Scots. By some accounts, during the reign of Caesar many a Roman could be seen hacking away. They would whittle branches into clubs and strike feather-stuffed balls. This, when not out conquering countries or turning Chinese noodles into spaghetti.

Several books show Dutch men playing a golf-like game on frozen canals during the fifteenth century. Crazy people are still playing cold weather golf, as you will see in the "Variations of the Game We Love" chapter. In addition, I've included a description of pasture golf. This version of the game is more common than canal golf and was played by the Scots as well as hackers in

France and Belgium.[2] Even here in the United States, early rounds were played on fallow fields.

In Scotland, though, golf could not be played during times of war. This, because open spaces were needed for archery practice and also because King James II didn't want his warriors wasting their time playing with their putters. Bows and arrows, boys! Bows and arrows!!! It was in 1457 that golf—or, as the Scots spelled it, "gowf" or "goff"—was outlawed as the country geared up to defend itself against England. For a while, the church also had a problem with the game as it took time away from religious ceremony, but then somebody invited a man of the cloth out for a round and all was forgiven (even if the debate rages on between God-fearing wives and golf-loving husbands on any given Sunday!).

But that's not to say that golf is a man's game. Long before Annika Sorenstam and Michelle Wie, the world's most famous lady golfer was Mary, Queen of Scots. Don't think for a moment, though, that she hit pink golf balls. No, not our Mary. She was actually seen laughing while playing a round at Seton Fields in 1565, just days after the murder of her husband, Lord Darnley. Now does that sound like the kind of woman who's going to play from the red tees? I don't think so. More the stuff of legend than history is the tale of how golf was transformed from a nine-hole game to eighteen holes. Apparently, Mary had lost a round at St. Andrews and so she demanded "a second nine." Unfortunately for her opponents, she lost that round, too. And so what does one do when one is not just a weekend warrior, but a maniacal monarch? Off with their heads!

---

[2] A "hacker" is a golfer bad enough to celebrate a bogey; a weekend warrior with a wanted poster hanging in his honor in post offices and pro shops alike. "Wanted: for the murder of a fellow golfer with a terrible tee shot." This is the typical hacker, a guy just like you and me!

Mary, although she was Queen of Scotland, was French. Whenever she played she brought along a couple of French soldiers, or cadets, to help her find her ball, choose a club, wave down the Beverage Girl, and discuss important events like the last episode of *Desperate Housewives*. But I had a point here. And that point is: as cadet is a French word, Mary gets credit for creating the word "caddy."[3] Further proof that golf is a game for everyone, from men to women, butchers to queens. Speaking of the hallowed grounds of St. Andrews, it is widely regarded as one of the world's oldest golf courses with tales of its use dating back to the sixteenth century. The Royal and Ancient Golf Club at St. Andrews was officially founded in 1754 and is just one of the many places I would like to play before following Ernie up to the Great Green in the Sky.

MY DREAM COURSES

5. The West Course at Winged Foot: Mamaroneck, New York, is less than thirty miles from my place of birth and to play where so many fantastic professionals have played would be an honor and a privilege. Walk into any clubhouse in America and you're guaranteed to see some sort of print, painting, or lithograph of Ben Hogan at Winged Foot. Perhaps some day you will see Sir Slice-A-Lot at the seventeenth tee.

4. Club de Golf Valderrama: I have been to Spain but have never played this course, once the host of the Ryder Cup. To be able to enjoy the *poniente* (hot summer wind) and the *levante* (the cooler sea breeze coming off of the Mediterranean), to try and conquer the *poniente* and the *levante* . . . *Bueno*.

---

[3] *I actually don't enjoy playing with a caddy. Although I like having help when lining up a putt, I get twice as angry after a bad shot, knowing that this guy thinks I suck. Which I do, but I don't need somebody thinking it at the same time as me!*

3. Pebble Beach: In my office hangs a flag and a postcard from the Left Coast's premier golf course. Jack Nicklaus once said, "If I only had one round to play, I'd play it at Pebble Beach." Good enough for me!

2. The Old Course at the Royal and Ancient Golf Club at St. Andrews. This goes without saying, but I'll say it anyway. Local legend has it that golf was being played here one hundred years before Christopher Columbus crossed the Atlantic and more than two hundred years before Shakespeare penned his first play. Romeo, Romeo . . . Wherefore art thy ball, Romeo?

1. Augusta National: It was in 1955 that Arnold Palmer made his debut here, at The Masters. How long till I make my debut?!?! It is at Augusta that one will find golf's infamous Amen Corner, three of the toughest holes you could ever hope to conquer.[4] I scored an eighteen at World Tour Golf Links replica of Amen Corner, a mere six-over par for the par-4 eleventh, par-3 twelfth, and par-5 thirteenth. That's some top-notch golf, baby! The folks at World Tour even thought to include Rae's Creek, but I still want to play the real deal.

Augusta is famous for its beauty and traditions—none more so than the Green Jacket. This is the "trophy" given to the winning golfer in a ceremony that dates back to 1937. Members were urged to wear green jackets during the Masters Tournament so that guests would know who to approach with questions. In 1949, the first Green Jacket was awarded, going to that year's champion, Sam Snead. As tradition would have it, the winning golfer takes his Green Jacket home with him for one year, returning it

---

[4] In a 1958 Sports Illustrated article, Herbert Warren Wind named this formidable trio of holes after a jazz song by Milton "Mezz" Mezzrow, "Shouting in the Amen Corner."

at the start of the following year's Masters Tournament. The Jacket is stored there and is available whenever the golfer comes back to play. A multiple winner has just one Green Jacket unless, of course, his size changes. No more onion rings for that guy!

Another of the Masters traditions is for the winner from the previous year to present the Green Jacket to the new champ. Before media, family, friends, and fellow golfers, the old welcomes in the new by helping him to put on the Green Jacket. In 1966, Jack Nicklaus put on his own coat as the first repeat winner. When it comes to Augusta, that man doesn't need any help.

I would love to hit Augusta National for the Masters. Any of the golf courses listed above, for that matter! Of course I want to play them, but I'd be willing to settle for a guest pass to take in a tournament. This side of the Big Pond or the other, just to see the game's greatest players would be a dream come true. The birth of the big tournament came on October 17, 1860, in Ayrshire, Scotland. It was at the Prestwick Golf Club that the first-ever British Open was held. Soon thereafter, tournaments and golf clubs sprang up across the globe. In 1873, Canada's Royal Montreal Club was established, thus becoming North America's first golf club. Fifteen years later, another St. Andrews was founded, in Yonkers, New York. It was only a three-hole course, but still gets credit as the first golf club in the U.S. Originally constructed on a cow pasture, the founders of St. Andrews became known as the "Apple Tree Gang" when they expanded into an apple orchard, making it a six-hole course. The first eighteen-hole course was the Chicago Golf Club, which opened for business in 1893.

One year after the Chicago Golf Club opened up shop, the USGA came into existence. This is the group that rules on the aforementioned ball specifications, although much more time is spent now on the golf clubs themselves. In 1916, the Professional Golfers' Association of America (PGA) was established, following the lead of a sister organization in Great Britain. One of the traditions to blossom from this kinship is the Ryder Cup competition. Every other year, a team from the American PGA plays against a team from the British PGA. The first match was played in 1927 and is named after the man who proposed it, Samuel Ryder. Ryder, a big golfer and even bigger businessman, planted the seeds for one of golf's greatest rivalries, which only makes sense as he'd made all of his money inventing those small packets still used to sell seeds today.

Hacker Facts

If you can play a course designed by one of the following fellows, consider yourself lucky: Bob Cupp, Tripp Davis, Pete Dye, Tom Fazio, Hale Irwin, Rees Jones, Robert Trent Jones, Alister MacKenzie, Jack Nicklaus, Greg Norman, Arnold Palmer, Gary Player, Donald Ross, Arthur Warren Tillinghast, and Tom Weiskopf.

It wasn't until the leisure days of the 1920s that tournament golf became a big-time spectator sport and it swept the nation like today's Texas Hold'em craze. Robert Trent Jones, Jr. won five U.S. Amateur titles, four U.S. Opens, and three British Opens during this decade, helping to spread word of the game. There was a slight decline in the 1930s and 40s as some people opted for poverty, famine, and war over tee times and tournaments. But in the 1950s, folks got their priorities back in order. As prize money increased, so did the game's popularity. The emergence of Arnold Palmer and Jack Nicklaus didn't hurt, either. As time went by, the money itself became newsworthy: in 1988, Curtis Strange became the first golfer to win more than one million dollars. The Professional Golfers' Association (PGA) tour is now to golf what the NFL is to football and there's even a Golf Channel on cable.[5] The game has certainly come a long way from the days of cow pastures, beheadings, the Great Depression, and 3:00 AM wake-up calls.

---

[5] As further proof of modern-day popularity, the Golf Channel even produces a reality show called The Big Break.

2

The Basics: An Introductory Course

Irst things first: the golf clubs. Like Thor's hammer and Zorro's sword, Hendrix's guitar and Bill Gates's mouse, these are your weapons, man. Wield wisely and wield well!!! When I got that starter set from my folks, I went for the hammer first. Instinctively, I pulled out the big dog, the driver, and it's a habit I'm still trying to break. And I know I'm not the only one. It's just something about men . . . We can't help but be drawn to the biggest club in the bag.[6] Needless to say, for the rookies out there I will describe the driver first and then work my way up to the wedges.

[6] *Would Freud call this driver envy?!?*

FROM THE DRIVER TO THE PUTTER

1. Driver: With a loft that's never more than thirteen degrees, the ball is always teed up. The driver is hit off of the tee box only and because the shaft is so long (mine is forty-three inches, thank you very much), this is often the hardest club for inexperienced golfers to control.

2. Fairway woods: There are 3-, 5-, 7-, and 9-woods. (As with irons, the degree/severity of the loft rises with the number.) You can hit one of these off of the tee box, but they will most often be played from the fairway. Thus, the name. Actually, who'm I kidding? These woods, especially the seven and nine, are often referred to not as fairway woods but as "rescue woods" because after you've screwed up your drive, you need to hit a great shot from the rough to save your score. These woods can help.

3. Three- and four-irons: I think that these are *the* toughest clubs to hit. Although the shaft may be shorter than the woods, the flat, thin, minimal-loft club head leaves little room for error. If you can hit one of these well, you will get tremendous distance. For my money, I'd rather just hit a nice easy 3-wood.

4. Crap club: I have an old club in my bag for hitting off of rocks and roots. It's a 3-iron and I use it to punch out of the rough, the bushes, the fescue, and back onto the fairway. I used to carry a lefty 3-iron and just now realized I haven't seen that club in five or six years!

5. Five-, six-, seven-irons: Determining distance is a personal thing. For example, my man ButtNut hits his 5-iron as far as I hit my 7-iron. Unfortunately, he hits his straight while I do not. These middle irons are relatively easy to control and provide a comforting combination of distance and loft. What

you use where, especially on par 3s, will depend on what kind of distance you get. The more you play, the more you will understand your game, the better judgment you'll have in terms of distance and club selection.[7]

6. Eight- and nine-irons: If you're holding one of these, the green is within sight, my friend! Usually, these clubs are good for golfers standing one hundred to one hundred and fifty yards away from the pin. The shorter shaft provides greater control and many golfers, present company included, open up the front foot a little. As you will see in Chapter 6, "Shaving Some Strokes," the ball should be closer to your back foot when hitting these shorter-shaft approach shots.

7. Pitching wedge, lob wedge, and sand wedge: The difference between each of these is the degree of loft. At this point, the shaft doesn't get any shorter, but you will choose a club depending on how high you want your ball to go or, to state the obvious, whether or not your ball has taken a detour to the beach! I do not carry a lob wedge, but have a nice 56-degree Cleveland that The Jimmy gave me for being a groomsman in his wedding. That alone made the tux rental worth it!

8. Putter: Like mini golf, except you'll be cursing at this one more.

I carry fourteen clubs in my bag as this is the legal limit on most courses and in most associations. Each club is different and requires a different mind set. In Chapter 6, I provide illustrations to make clear where the ball should be at address: just remember

---

[7] *And don't feel badly when you make a bad choice. For one, the pros use caddies. And secondly, often times course managers will "tweak" their yardage markers to make the course appear longer than it is. As if judging distance wasn't hard enough . . .*

that I'm speaking for myself and that you should adjust to your own liking. Look at each of the other golfers in your foursome and you're liable to see a variety of set-ups at address. Watch other golfers and learn. It's the best way—better, even, than reading some goofy book!

3

The Basics:
An Advanced Course

Ernie's Thundering Herd included men who'd been playing golf for over fifty years. In my own version of The Thundering Herd, we have a couple of guys who can't break fifty on the front nine. These are hackers who'd only played a handful of times before Y2K! To their credit, though, they've been bitten by the bug and are now in the throes of the addiction that is golf. They're buying equipment and studying up on the rules; learning what all of the different phrases mean and figuring out a way to get out to play more often. They are starting with the basics and working their way towards improvement. So, in honor of all of the rookies out there, I'd like to offer up a quick refresher.

Why is it that you have to play in a foursome? I don't know. Despite all of my nosing around, I couldn't find a reference for the origins of the foursome. Chances are, it had something to do with Mary, Queen of Scots! Regardless, a foursome is launched from the starter's booth once every eight minutes or so, out of consideration for the pace of play. Better golf courses wait a little longer, to avoid injury from incoming missiles launched by the foursome behind. Despite the familiarity of the foursome, you can still play even if you don't have three playing partners. Rangers and starters are very good at pairing people up, so that the maximum number of golfers can get out on the course on any given day.

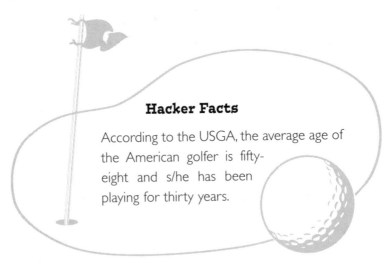

Hacker Facts

According to the USGA, the average age of the American golfer is fifty-eight and s/he has been playing for thirty years.

The longer a round takes, the fewer golfers who can play. And pay! So, it is in everybody's interest to *not* have seven-hour rounds. Public (or municipal) courses are notorious for long weekend rounds. But I'd say it's safe to expect a golf outing on a Saturday or Sunday to take you no more than six hours, depending on how busy the course is. At a private course, or a lesser-played muni, it's reasonable to expect to be on and off in five hours. Vacation golf at a resort usually means a time closer to four hours.

The length and difficulty of the golf course also play a part in determining how long the round will last. Ninety-nine-point-nine percent of eighteen-hole golf courses are somewhere between 6,000 and 7,000 yards in length. This number will vary, of course, depending on which tees you choose to hit from. Most men will play from the whites, unless they are very good. The red tees are for women. Gold and black tees are for championship play, while blue tees fall between these—way back, like in another zip code!—and the white tees. If a foursome has four players of varying skill and gender, it's no big deal. Whoever is hitting from the furthest tee hits first. Rather than "honoring" the player with the best score on the previous hole, you proceed in a more polite, common-sense, "ready play" fashion. And no need to be embarrassed if you go out by yourself and get paired with three guys playing from the golds. You'd rather be good (and speedy) off of the whites than slow (and painful to play with!) from the golds.

It's harder to peg the price per round than it is the time it will take, as an area's cost of living comes into play. Just know that not only is weekend golf more time consuming, it's also more cash consuming. If you can get in a twilight round (usually after 3:00 PM) during the week that will probably be the cheapest round you can find. It's also less expensive if you walk, rather than take a cart. (Many courses require a cart on the weekends, in order to speed up play.) Call ahead if you're going to try and play a twilight, weekday round, though, as many public courses host leagues. If you're looking for folks to play with, you can probably get into one of these leagues.

Not only do I enjoy the peace, quiet, and camaraderie of a round of golf, I like the food. That's right: the food! A decent course will find creative ways to take more of your money, so in addition to the bar and grill at the nineteenth hole, you will hopefully have purchasing options while playing. There may be a snack shack between the ninth and tenth holes—commonly referred to as The Turn—providing the sustenance to see you through the back nine. Many a round has been augmented by a cold beer or three, and a candy bar. The golf courses I love most, though, go a step further. Mobile refreshments, my friends. That's right: a Beverage Girl.

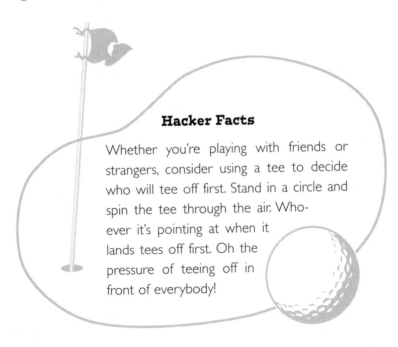

Hacker Facts

Whether you're playing with friends or strangers, consider using a tee to decide who will tee off first. Stand in a circle and spin the tee through the air. Whoever it's pointing at when it lands tees off first. Oh the pressure of teeing off in front of everybody!

I shall not tell a lie: the prices for food and drink are generally one step below highway robbery, so if you're looking to put away a six-pack, I'd suggest packing your own cooler. Some courses allow it, while others do not. If it's against the rules and you try it anyway, and some savvy starter questions you, do the dishonorable thing and lie. If you're an honest fellow, this might be difficult, but if you're thirsty enough, you'll do what's necessary. Just think of it as a little white lie. . . . Not that I have done it myself, but I've heard guys say that they are diabetic when the starter tries to bust them. Starters, by their nature, don't like to leave their little booths and don't want any trouble. Just be somewhat convincing and they'll let the cooler pass. You'll have your beer. (Just don't crack one open while telling your little white lie!)

So now, let's say you're not just a golf rookie, but a golfing virgin. You've never, ever been out on the course, but it seems like the game might be to your liking. Fear not the expense. Like me with my starter set from Caldor's, it is possible to get all you need for under $300. As you improve, you can upgrade your equipment. I did it with golf just as I did it with guitar. Until I'd taken a few lessons and learned some chords and scales, I was purely acoustic. But then . . . the Fender! The amp!! The wah-wah pedal!!! You'll buy that big-headed driver someday, but until you've learned the ins and outs, be happy with what you've got. Get out there and start hacking. Amateur championships await!

Speaking of which, the Dupont World Amateur Handicap Championship, held in Myrtle Beach, is the largest handicap championship in the country. Over the course of four days, more than 4,000 golfers play on more than seventy-five courses, competing for $500,000 in prizes. Weekend warrior hacker heaven, but not without its worries. Given the size of the field, it's no surprise that there have been problems over the years with "questionable" handicaps. Although tournament director Bob Mazzone and his staff use a thorough system to weed out sandbaggers, he admits that there's only so much that can be done. "With the numbers we deal with, it's a logistical nightmare."

But imagine the nightmare if there were no systems? If no one had ever heard of handicaps? Of sandbaggers? Of slope and par and Beverage Girl and *Caddyshack*? It boggles the mind!

Perhaps you've never heard of handicaps and sandbaggers and slope and par and Beverage Girl. That's fine. Just please tell me you've heard of *Caddyshack*. Please! If you can lie about being diabetic, you can lie about the greatest movie ever conceived by brothers.

Anyway, here's a closer look at how golfers track their progress and how tournament officials track cheaters:

Score

Definition: **1.** the number of points made in a game by a player or team; a successful move or stroke **2.** the act of getting or stealing **3.** to have sexual intercourse.

Well, forget the sex and forget everything you know about scoring well in sports. Golf is unlike any other game you've ever played. Despite what your friends tell you before your virgin round, you don't want the highest score at the end of the day. This isn't bowling!

Par

Definition: **1.** the number of golf strokes necessary to complete a hole or entire course by an expert **2.** an amount considered to be average.[8] The origin: Long before golf was a sport, par was a word. Away from the course, it means average, while on the course it is only average for the most excellent of golfers. Of note is the fact that when par was first used in golf, it meant the same thing as the already-existent bogey.[9] Over time, as more and more hackers took up the sport, bogey migrated north, equating average for the average golfer. One worse than excellent. One worse than par.

---

[8] *Average, my ass! I think that I "average" like one or two pars per round!!!*

[9] *Bogey is, for those not yet in the know, one above par. If par is 4 and you shoot a 5, that's bogey. If an eighteen-hole course is a par 72 and you shoot a 90, that's bogey golf. I'd gladly take that.*

In 1905, a fellow named Leighton Calkins, the secretary of the Metropolitan Golf Association, decided to use the play of U.S. Amateur champion, Jerome Travers, to develop a par rating system. Travers would play a course and his score would determine par for that course. If I'd been hired for the job, we'd all be much happier: the land would be filled with courses where par ranges from 92 to 102! Calkins kept that in mind, writing, "The principal feature of this system is that not only is the good player handicapped because he is a good player, but the bad player is also handicapped because he is a bad player." In 1947, the Calkins/Travers system was combined with a system already in use in Massachusetts and holes were now rated in "tenths of a stroke." To make it clear for course managers, *The Handicap Manual* was developed, providing descriptions that typified holes of a specific rating. The ratings for all of the holes would be totaled up and then rounded off to the nearest whole number. Anyone else feel lost?

In 1960, as courses grew longer and longer (because those rhino snot balls could be hit farther and farther), yardage became a much more important factor and the system was adjusted. Meanwhile, in Great Britain, the term "scratch player" was being widely used to describe someone who frequently shot par; someone who, in the U.S., would have a handicap of 0. Mind you, nowadays nobody is referred to as having a "zero handicap." Across the pond, we, too, call them scratch golfers.

Handicap

Definition: **1.** a contest in which different compensations are given to different players to equalize the chances of winning **2.** to have a disability, such as the inability to read . . . a green. The origin: from "hand in cap," an obsolete game in which forfeits were picked out of a cap.

Here's how the USGA's GHIN (Golfer's Handicap Index) works: if you have the Internet, they'll figure out your handicap (or the measure of how good/bad you are) for you. All you have to do is input a couple of numbers.[10] You will be asked to record your scores, keeping in mind the stroke limit that I will explain shortly. You will also be asked for the length of the course from the tees that you played. In terms of stroke limit, you can't ever record a score higher than net double bogey on any hole. Let's say you're a fifteen handicap (meaning that you average fifteen-above-par whenever you play) playing a par 4 hole that is ranked as the twelfth hardest hole on the course. You finish the hole with an eight, but can only take, according to the rules, a seven: this net double bogey includes an adjusted par of five—meaning plus one to account for your fifteen handicap—plus the maximum double bogey of two over par for a seven. Until you've played enough rounds to determine an actual handicap, simply guesstimate what net double bogey would be for you on each hole. If you're thinking you might be an eighteen handicap, you get to add a stroke on each hole. If you're thinking you might be a fifteen, as in the example above, only add a stroke on the fifteen hardest holes.

I'll mention now that every hole on the course is ranked in relation to the other seventeen holes. The number-one handicap hole is the hardest hole on the course. In this way, you see that handicap actually has two different meanings for golfers. As confusing as learning to speak English is this game! But hey, Ernie learned to do both . . .

After posting your first score, you'll have a handicap based on that one score. And after you've posted your next four scores, your handicap will be based on the second-best score. When you

---

[10] *Honest numbers, unlike your beer-based diabetes!*

have six, seven, eight, or nine scores recorded, your handicap will be based on the average of your second and third-best scores. And after you've posted ten-plus scores, your handicap will be based on the average of your second-, third- and fourth-best differentials of the *last* ten rounds played. A differential is score minus the course rating, calculated to the nearest tenth. That average becomes your GHIN. Contrary to what rookies and weekend warrior hackers lacking in tournament experience might expect, the best score is not used because every golfer is allowed one great score (commonly referred to as a "career round") without it unfairly reducing your handicap.

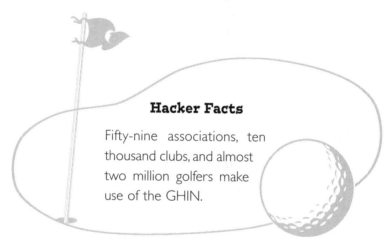

Hacker Facts

Fifty-nine associations, ten thousand clubs, and almost two million golfers make use of the GHIN.

Now, all of that is fine and good, but it isn't the only way. Here's how I determine my handicap. At round's end, I look at my score for each hole and especially at how many putts it took to finish. If I putted out in two or less, I subtract one stroke from my overall score. If I had to three-putt (or worse), I punch myself in the kidney. Then I subtract two strokes. I also track my imbibing for the round, cigars included. Each beer equates one subtracted stroke from the total. Each cigar means I get to subtract three. And yes, I have been known to enjoy one on the front and one on the back. As a fair-minded golfer such as yourself would expect, I subtract for both stogies: six strokes gone, just like that.

Through this take-away system, I not only get my score, I'm able to determine my handicap, which is . . . two. OK, so it's actually a twenty-four. I forgot to mention that when there's no money on the table, I never take more than an eight on a hole. By limiting myself to the proverbial snowman, I'm able to continue living life as a happy, well-balanced, non-postal person. I'm able to stay interested in the round. I'm able to have civil discourse with friends I see far too infrequently. I'm able to approach subsequent shots with confidence. Confidence, after all, is half the battle. Of this, I am sure. I think.

Hacker Facts

In 1900, it was the Ladies Golf Union (LGU) that gave the game its first handicapping system. In *A History of Golf,* Robert Browning writes, "No doubt it was uphill work at the start, but within eight or ten years the LGU had done what the men had failed to do—established a system of handicapping that was reasonably reliable from club to club."

Slope

Definition: **1.** a rating system that allows golfers to know just how difficult a golf course is going to be so that they can put their clubs back into their trunk and go home because the grass does need to be cut and there are many better uses of time; better than hacking away for six hours on holes that are way too difficult **2.** to diverge from the vertical or horizontal; an incline; a slant; to ascend or descend. The origin: The mind of The Pope of Slope.

The slope system is a refinement of the USGA Handicap System. It adjusts a player's handicap for the difficulty of the course he is playing. In theory, a scratch golfer should shoot a 70 on a course with a 70 rating; a 72 on a course with a 72 rating. But when you or I or any other golfer with a twenty-four handicap plays a really tough course, our score tends to rise more than the difference in course ratings. I might shoot a 100 on a 72 course, but that's okay because the slope system accounts for this. It also does the same, in reverse, accounting for the golfer who builds his handicap at a very difficult course and scores well below it when he plays on easier courses.

By basing the rating on a mathematical formula derived from the scores of various golfers of various handicaps playing on courses of varying difficulty, fairness is achieved. In a nutshell, the slope is the relative difficulty of a course for a bogey player in comparison to a scratch player. As *Golf Digest's* Bob Carney describes it, "If one were to plot a graph of these scores for any given course, it would be a line which 'slopes' up from left to right . . . The steeper the slope, the higher the Slope Rating."

There is a man out there, a thinkin' man's thinkin' man, and he is known as The Pope of Slope. In 1977, this man (real name, Dean Knuth) developed the slope rating system for the USGA. You didn't think they'd nickname him Pope for something less significant than that, did you?

The Pope's system made use of ten criteria for rating a hole. According to his website (*www.popeofslope.com*), "The method used some elements of decision theory and was intended to be a systematic, quantitative approach to course rating." The following ten features are a part of the rating process: topography (how level the landing area is and the vertical angle of the shot up to the green), fairway (width and depth of the landing area, with consideration for doglegs, trees, and fairway slope), recoverability and rough, out-of-bounds, water hazards, trees (location, size, height, and number), bunkers (in the proximity of the landing area and around the green), green target (size, firmness, shape, and slope of the green), green surface (contour and normal speed of the putting surface), and finally, my favorite, psychological factors (mental effect that obstacles may have, in relation to the target areas). Some serious psychological damage has been inflicted on me by par 3s. So easy on the eye, so hard on the score. Woe is me.

Tom Dellner writes, "Ask your club professional to explain the USGA Slope System and you'll hear him assume the tone of a weary sixth-grade teacher trying to explain the New Math." But this didn't stop the concept from spreading.

The Colorado Golf Association took a leadership role when, in 1982, they adjusted the ratings for each of the state's 110 courses. They decided to document and analyze all away scores and the results showed that by using the slope system, the average error in handicapping was reduced from three strokes to six-tenths of a stroke. As the range of tournament scores shrank, entry requests increased. Suddenly, all was fair in love, war, and golf!

News of Colorado's success spread to other associations. In 1983, five more associations slope-rated their courses. By 1985, the number had jumped to twenty, and then, by 1987, to sixty-five. (While Duran Duran rocked, Colorado's golf courses rolled!)

In California, these days, each course is re-rated every seven years. And of the nation's 12,000 courses, 10,000 have been re-rated. The slope system is an attempt by the authorities to deliver golf and golf tournament play to the average joe, fair and square. The more it spreads, the more tournaments there shall be!

"The amazing thing about it," The Pope of Slope says, "is that the system has completely sold itself. We've never made any effort to market slope."

Of course, there are some resisters. Augusta National doesn't provide a course rating as they feel each of its *exclusive* members already know the handicaps of their fellow members. Thankfully, the folks at *Golf Digest* refused to be denied. They used highly qualified volunteers to rank the course and it emerged as one of the toughest in the U.S. According to Ross Goodner, who put together the article, the green surface ratings for the average U.S. Open course is 110, compared to Augusta's 148 (and you won't find any slicker than that). No wonder Hootie Johnson handled Martha Burke with such ease.[11]

On the subject, Ko'olau Golf Course in Hawaii, and not Pine Valley in New Jersey (with its 153 slope rating), is the world's most difficult golf course. The Pope of Slope himself gave Ko'olau a rating of 155. Aloha means hello *and* goodbye!

Sandbagger

Now, a look at those who are still trying to make golf *un*fair. The definition: **1.** one who downplays or misrepresents his ability in a game (especially when gambling is involved), in order to deceive **2.** one who forces by crude means; coerces **3.** one who treats others unjustly **4.** one who has won in a way that one is not

---

[11] *Those greens . . . Amen Corner . . . NOW . . . Being confused with Darius Rucker . . . I don't know how Hootie does it.*

supposed to. The origin: From a bag filled with sand that is used not to keep back water but to beat someone over the head.

As a function of the Department of Homeland Security, in conjunction with the CIA, the FBI, and the IRS, a profile has been established for sandbaggers. Although this early warning system does not yet include a color-coded schematic, it is useful for anyone running a tournament. Employing the tracking system of the GHIN, scores for thousands of golfers were analyzed, allowing local law enforcement to ID those who always somehow play better in tournaments than their handicaps would predict. The numbers indicate that only .15 percent of all golfers sandbag. (Then again, the percentage of golfers signing up for big-money tournaments and member-guest club championships is probably pretty low, too.) On average, sandbaggers list their handicap as twenty. One story even has a guy trying to sell his handicap as forty-three! Your run-of-the-mill golfer plays twenty-one rounds per year, but sandbaggers will only claim to have played eight rounds; signing up for tourneys left and right but playing less than ten times a year. The truth is, they are playing much more, but posting less than half their scores.

According to Tom Ridge, when tournament time comes, your average sandbagger will beat his handicap by at least six strokes. Can you say, "WARNING SIGN!!!"? The mathematicians inform me that the majority of golfers will only beat their handicap by more than two strokes once over the course of twenty rounds. To go a step further, fewer than 9 percent of golfers ever beat their handicap by six strokes. Sandbaggers not only accomplish this rare feat, they manage to do it *only* in tournaments. Hmmmm . . .

Bill Gates was once purportedly involved in a sandbagging scandal. He of all people should understand the culpability, the implications when the math doesn't add up.

Everyone cheats when they first start playing golf. A lot of people don't ever stop!

—*Frank Beard*

At a charity tournament in Seattle, Gates shot an 87. He did so despite claiming a handicap of thirty. Combine that score and *that* handicap and Gates easily finished the low net winner for the tournament. His prize: a $58 billion fortune. The Pope of Slope, when informed of what Gates had done, hopped onto the prosecutorial bandwagon faster than Elliot Ness. "That's statistically impossible," he said. "A 30 cannot shoot an 87. He cannot." I'm no math wizard, Mr. Gates, but here are some numbers even I can understand. According to The Pope, the odds of beating your handicap by three strokes are just one in 200. By five strokes? We're talking one in 570. Ten under? The odds increase to one in 82,000. Gates beat his supposed handicap by fifteen strokes. Fifteen! Come on, computer boy. We know you're competitive, but . . .[12]

U.S. intelligence has gotten wise to vanity handicappers, as well. These guys are sometimes called "reverse sandbaggers." They cheat not for money, but for love and respect. Vanity

---

[12] *In fairness to Bill, he did just donate three-quarters of a billion dollars to inoculate poor children, all around the world, against sickness and sandbaggers.*

handicappers only post their best scores. Or worse, they out-and-out cheat, posting scores better than what they actually shot. They're not worried about sharking anybody in tournament play. They simply want to appear to be excellent golfers.

The Pope of Slope says, "Vanity handicappers are just delusional optimists, though they are terrible partners to be stuck with." Delusional optimists . . . I think that the world would be a better place with more optimists. Not necessarily delusional, but glass-half-full will do.

When I first started playing, I was a cheater. Sometimes I would tee the ball up in the rough to give myself a cleaner shot. Other times, I'd be so embarrassed by a score that I'd shave a stroke or three to save face. But I will say this: never, ever did I cheat when there was money on the line. As I will soon describe, golf offers many wonderful opportunities for betting. Just remember, it's hard to swing a club with a broken thumb. Let's keep it clean, people. No cheatin' when bettin' and no squelchin' when losin'!

4

Banter

One of the things I love most about hanging with my boys is the talk. Even those Thundering Herdsters who're new to golf have a certain acumen when it comes to dissin' and discussin'. A fortunate few even possess both: the gift of gab *and* game.

Golf is a lifelong endeavor. And as long as I've been playing, each time out it still seems as if I learn something new. For example, down in Myrtle Beach, a friend by the name of Dr. Dave taught me about elephant ass. After I hit an 8-iron too high and too short on an easy-to-reach par 3, he said that my shot was "elephant ass." No, despite the recent expansion of my derriere, he wasn't calling *me* "elephant ass." He was referring to my lame attempt at landing the green which was, as he explained, "High and stinky!" Handed down from his father to him to me and now to you. High and stinky: elephant ass.[13]

At Myrtle Beach's World Tour Golf Links, Dr. Dave and Johnny Mac "traveled" to Spain's Valderrama for a photo with a waterfall-lovin' wood stork. Even banter takes a break at breathtaking holes like this. What can you say other than muy bonita?

For those of you who've yet to go out for a round, this is the kind of shop talk that you have to look forward to. And I promise, it doesn't take someone with a doctoral degree to share such wisdom!

So here now, gathered for your perusal, is a complete guide to the golfing vernacular. Take it in like a fine wine, my friends. Or, better yet, a cold beer and a hot dog at the nineteenth hole. Ah-hhhhhhhh. You will meet several members of my Thundering Herd—guys with names like The Jimmy, Egg Head, and Ish—as they help describe everything from "address" to the "yips." Ed Norton, Ernest Hemingway, and John Travolta will chip in, too!

[13] *The opposite would be a knock-down shot. Not easy to hit, this is a low line drive into the wind. We could call that one snake ass, I suppose.*

FORTY-THREE GOLF TERMS YOU'VE GOTTA KNOW OTHERWISE EVERYBODY FROM BEVERAGE GIRL TO CART HOSE-DOWN GUY WILL LAUGH AT YOU

1. Address: When the player gets into position to strike the ball. The most famous reference to address came in *The Honeymooners* episode when Ralph tried to teach Norton how to play golf. "Hello, ball!" was the punch line and is the second most-often used quote in all of golf.

2. Approach: A shot intended to reach the green. The most exciting shot to watch is the approach shot, from the decision to go for it to the club selection to the shot itself.

3. Away: The player farthest from the hole; he gets to shoot first. Sample sentence, in Hemingway style: "I was still away and the work was good. The cool of the dawn had run from the rising sun and so I gave my absinthe to the boy and stroked the ball once more. It was a bloody day but there was an understanding and that was enough."

4. Ball mark: The damage that a ball causes when it hits the ground (usually the putting green). It is good etiquette to repair any ball marks you may see on the green.

5. Birdie: A score of one-under-par on a hole. Tweet, tweet, tweet down on Sesame Street!

6. Bogey: A score of one-over-par on a hole. Bogey golf on a par 72 means a score of 90 and I'd happily settle for that. If only I could break 90 . . .

7. Break: The curves and slopes on a green. I need to learn how to read the breaks if my putting is to improve. If only Dr. Seuss had written a golf book!

8. Bunker: Any hollowed-out hazard, most often a sand trap. Many a suntan lotion reference will be made when you land in the "beach."

9. Carry: The distance a ball flies through the air. In the movie *Tin Cup*, Costner just couldn't carry the water.

10. Chili dip: A short chip or pitch shot that is not hit well, the ball going a much shorter distance than intended. Sample sentence, in Emeril style: "Nothin' like chili and dip, just not on the golf course. BAM!"

11. Chip: A shot that is supposed to roll farther than it flies. (Also known as a "bump and run.") A chip stays close to the ground and has less loft than a pitch.

12. Course management: The plan that a golfer has for scoring well on a particular course. If my man Ish cared even the least bit about course management, I'm sure he'd cut ten strokes off of his score. Easy.

13. Cup: The hole (diameter not to exceed 4.25 inches) you are aimin' for!

14. Dance floor: The green. Sample sentence, in Travolta style: "You see dat? Didjoo see dat?! I hit da ball on da dance floo'. Hey, watch da hair. Watch da hair!!!"

15. Divot: A chunk of turf ripped up from the ground the same way your heart is ripped from your chest every time your ball skitters out of bounds.[14]

16. Dogleg: A hole on which there is a drastic bend in the fairway, like the rear leg of a dog. When I used to be known as Sir Slice-A-Lot, I never minded holes with a dogleg to the right.

17. Drain: To sink a putt (usually one that is long and important and makes you feel like you really *are* a good golfer).

18. Fairway: The well-tended, well-mowed stretch of grass between the tee box and the green. A "Fairway in Regulation" (FIR) means your drive ended up on the fairway.

---

[14] *Depending on what kind of grass they've planted, some clubs will ask you to replace your divot while others will ask you to pour seed and sand.*

19. Flag: Also known as the pin, this is the thingy used to indicate where you should *never, ever* hit the ball. Only bad golfers aim for the flag and actually put their ball right next to it.

20. Fore: The word you should yell when your golf ball is about to clock a fellow golfer in the head.

21. Fringe: The short grass that separates the green from the rough or fairway (also known as the collar or apron). In a Closest to the Pin contest, a ball on the fringe cannot win.

22. Gimme: A putt that's so easy, the player is given permission to just pick it up and assume the final stroke. When people ask The Jimmy what his favorite shot is, he says, "The gimme." (And not because it rhymes with his name, either.)

23. Ground: Touching the sand with your club while preparing to hit out of a bunker. This is highly illegal and the punishment is an hour in the stockade where fellow golfers hurl obscenities and unwanted coleslaw at your shameful face.

24. Hacker: An unskilled golfer. No one has ever used this phrase around me. They prefer to wait till I'm out of the room.

25. Honor: The privilege of hitting first off of the tee, based on having the lowest score on the previous hole. This calls to mind the most-often quoted phrase in golf. Borrowed from *Caddyshack*, it is: "Your honor, Your Honor." Also referred to as "Away," meaning it's your turn to hit away.

26. Hook: A bad shot that moves, rather severely, from right to left (for right-handed players). I say rather severely because that's how my newfound hook comported itself this past summer. Yes, sports fans, I pulled the dreaded switcharoo, trading in my Sir Slice-A-Lot nickname for . . . Captain Hook.

27. Lay up: To hit the ball short, on purpose, so as to set up an easy chip. Maybe when I'm in my fifties or sixties I'll figure out that laying up is often the wisest shot to hit, but until then there is no siren song quite like the call of "Just go for it . . ."

28. Lie: a) Something Egg Head does whenever he reports his score; b) The ball in its position on the ground; c) The angle of the bottom of the club, where it meets the ground.

29. Mulligan: Taking a second shot after losing the first and not assessing a penalty stroke.[15] Whenever I'm playing and there's no money on the line, I like to offer a sociable mulligan on the front and another on the back.

30. Ninety degree: A rule that permits golf carts to drive onto the fairway, but only at a perpendicular angle from the cart path. Remember, the golf course is not Hazzard County and your cart is not the General Lee.

31. Out of bounds (OB): Any area that is out of play, usually marked with stakes (white, yellow, or red), fences, and stone walls. I often see more OB than FIR.

32. Par: The number of strokes in which a scratch player would be expected to complete a hole or course. (I had to look *this* definition up.)

33. Penalty stroke: A stroke added to the score after the ball goes out of bounds (or any of the other rules of the course). Sample sentence, in soap opera style: "Damn it, Jezebel, I *know* I have to take the penalty stroke. Can't you see what this is doing to me? I curse the day I met you. And . . . and I curse the day I ever picked up a golf club!" Now that's drama.

34. Picking up: Calling it quits on a hole to save time, energy, and/or face. Sometimes, picking up is the only way a beginning golfer can keep himself from getting too frustrated. Just take an 8 and move on.

---

[15] *This is my favorite shot, yet I call Egg Head a vanity sandbagger and The Jimmy a charity case!*

35. Play through: When one foursome lets another foursome go ahead, usually because they're playing too slow. Sometimes, a ranger will ask you to let a group play through, especially if they have less than four golfers.

36. Provisional: An additional shot that is hit when the first ball may be lost or out of bounds. Sample sentence, in Hallmark style: "The woods are so green/The water's so blue/Sometimes a provisional's/all you can do."[16]

37. Read: The act of surveying the line of a putt to determine its break and the speed necessary. Reading is fundamental . . .

38. Rough: The longer, cruddier, crappier, super duper unhappier grass surrounding the fairways and greens.

39. Slice: A curving shot that goes from left to right for a right-handed player. I had to look this definition up, too . . .

40. Snowman: A score of eight. I believe that unless you're tracking your handicap or playing for big money, this should be the maximum score (in order to keep from becoming suicidal). Sample sentence, in the holiday TV special style: "Frosty the Snowman is an ugly, nasty score. Made Ish unhappy, he got no golf clappy, just a chance to yell out, 'Foooore!'"

41. Swing oil: Any adult beverage consumed on the golf course. It can be tempting to skip entering your score after a round that includes all too much "swing oil," but when tracking your handicap, no excuses can be made. Feel free to imbibe while on the course, just don't complain when you shoot for the wrong green! (NOTE: As the Pope of Slope informs us, "The U.S. Golf Association Handicap System technically covers drugs and alcohol by stating that the system assumes a golfer will be playing his best at all times."

---

[16] *A provisional is a second, just-in-case tee shot, hit when you think you may have lost your first.*

42. Up and down: This describes a chip from just off the green followed by a one-putt, usually on a par 3. Nothing is more satisfying than getting up and down to save par.

43. Yardage marker: A landmark to tell golfers the distance to the green. Most often, you will find yardage markers in the middle of the fairway: blue for two hundred yards, white for one hundred and fifty yards, and red for one hundred yards.

I chose to include forty-three words and phrases because that's the lowest score I've ever recorded through nine. Wasn't that a cute idea? Well, I'll tell you what isn't cute: the fact that I proceeded to shoot a forty-nine on the back nine, ruining my one and only legitimate chance to break ninety. And so, I will give to you six more golf phrases, in honor of that back-nine blow up. Bonus banter, if you will.

44. Big Dog: An affectionate term for the driver, you'll hear many a hacker yell, "Bad dog! Bad dog!" after slicing one into the woods. (You may also hear a playing partner say, "Time to let the Big Dog eat" when he pulls his driver out for the first time that day.)

45. The Drink: Not refreshing whatsoever, to hit into The Drink is to put your ball into the water. Take a stroke and try again. If you're still mad about that first shot, though, you might want to *have* a drink before lining up another.

46. Golf clap: Save the loud clap for football games, hombre. Rather than slapping flat palm against flat palm as hard as you possibly can, as fast as you possibly can, simply cup your hands and let four fingers of one hand make contact, at the near-molasses speed of a dangerous downhill putt, with the palm of the other hand. Clap quietly and never more than four or five times. Then, pass the Grey Poupon because this, my friends, is etiquette!

47. Re-veg: The process of replacing and restoring all natural life damaged by your weedwacker of a golf swing. As simple as re-placing a divot on the fairway or as complex as bringing a near-extinct bush back to life after uprooting it for a better look at the green, to re-veg is to keep the balance between golf and Mother Nature intact.

48. Wormburner: A shot that barely gets off the ground, skimming along the grass at a rate of speed fast enough to scorch any worms that happen to wriggle into the ball's path.

49. Yips: To get a case of the yips is to lose your swing. And if it's your putting stroke, as is most often the case when the yips attack like the world's worst computer virus, it's to lose your mind!!!

So, I mentioned etiquette and the reintroduction of the golf clap . . . I know that both might be foreign concepts so, being the teacher that I am, I've provided a few real-life examples where this meeting of the hands might also be of use. I think you'll find that the golf clap feels as natural as a freshly made bed.

OTHER OPPORTUNITIES TO PRACTICE THE GOLF CLAP

1. As your boss exits the bathroom.

2. As the officer is writing out your ticket(s).

3. As the soccer mom pulls out in front of you, even though there's no one behind you, and then proceeds to go 15 miles per hour while on the cell phone. Better than road rage is the golf clap. And besides, did you really want to give the finger to somebody in a minivan?

4. As the pizza delivery guy waits for a tip, despite arriving an hour late . . . with a small plain when you'd ordered a large pepperoni!

5. As your son or daughter shows you a failing grade on the report card. This will surely confuse them as they prepare to launch into their excuse.

Did you know that etiquette is like the only word in the English dictionary that rhymes with Connecticut? With orange, too.

Etiquette is an important part of the game and it wasn't until I moved to Connecticut that I began to pay attention. This had nothing to do with the blue-blood nature of my new home state. No, it was because I'd matured. With a mortgage and a daughter, the idea of getting arrested for DWIing a golf cart into the caddyshack had lost some of its luster. Also, I figured it was time to stop wasting my money. If I was going to shell out for balls and greens fees, I might as well try and score. This required not only knowledge of proper golf etiquette, but of the rules.

You always want to know the rules; what's out of bounds and what marks the various hazards; what the distance markers are (from the green); whether or not you can drive the cart on the fairways; if there's a system for determining where the pin is on the green. Review the rules before teeing off. It might just save you a stroke or two.

A SAMPLE OF THE RULES
(FROM THE MYRTLEWOOD GOLF CLUB)

1. No gambling.[17]
2. Red stakes and lines mark lateral hazards.

---

[17] *No wait, that was Bushwood. (Sorry, I've tried to minimize the gratuitous "Caddyshack" references!)*

3. Yellow stakes and lines mark water hazards.

4. Please keep carts fifty feet from tees and greens. (An attempt to deter guys from combining golf and NASCAR.)

5. Ping markers indicate distance to front, center, and back of green.

6. Please repair all ball marks.

7. Dress code in effect, proper attire required.

8. Restrooms and water fountains are available on holes five, nine, thirteen, and fifteen.

9. Snack bar facilities available at The Turn.

We also played a much nicer course called World Tour Golf Links. This is the place that features Amen Corner and twenty-four other holes—each amongst the finest in the world. To get out and play on a course this nice, you must also adhere to a dress

Egg Head tries to chip in on this postage stamp of an island green, an amazing replica from Sawgrass. Notice how he keeps his (egg) head down. Notice how The Jimmy and Phat Head Andy resist reminding him that he is surrounded by water.

code. Whereas public golf courses look the other way, allowing patrons to wear cut-off shorts and tank tops, this is not the case at the classier joints and it certainly wasn't what we found at World Tour. To play the seventeenth island hole at Sawgrass, to try and conquer Amen Corner, you must be in proper attire, meaning Bermuda-length shorts and collared shirt; soft spike golf shoes, too. Leave the "ONE MARTINI, TWO MARTINI, THREE MARTINI, FLOOR!!!" shirt at home.

At both of these courses, you can rent golf clubs. Now me, being the good friend that I am, I hauled two sets of clubs down to Myrtle. One for me and one for the bachelor. After traveling with my baby girl, two sets of clubs was a piece of cake! Besides, it saved us at least $150. Tuppa traveled from Africa for the weekend, so it was the least I could do. A golf glove, balls, tees, and a ball marker, too.

And on that note, we shall now make the seamless transition from golf banter to golf gear.

5

Got Gear?

So there we were, ten men gathered for four days and three nights of fun in the sun. It was the second trip down to Myrtle Beach for The Thundering Herd and on that first night, all agreed: from now on, this would be a yearly thing. Yes, that most lauded of manly phrases: a tradition. This, because the die-hards want it and because the newly anointed need it.

That's right, just as my parents infected me, a couple of my buddies have recently been indoctrinated. In particular, there is Mr. Elephant Ass himself, Dr. Dave. Before the fall of 2004, he averaged one or two rounds a year and so never bothered to buy a set of clubs. Now that he has finished his post-doctoral work, though, now that he has the two kids, two dogs, a house with a picket fence and a supersafe minivan, now that he is struggling to find athletic competition like the rest of us, he was ready to learn the game. He was ready for his own set of clubs.

You have to be careful when purchasing your gear. If golf is going to be less of an infatuation and more of a lifelong endeavor, well then you can add to your bag over time. If you do it all at once, ringing up a monster of a bill, your frustration is liable to be even greater as improvement, top of the line clubs or not, is always slow in coming. So, do as Dr. Dave is doing. Do as I did.

I had that Caldor's starter set for five or six years before upgrading to a slightly better set of used irons. To this day, I've yet to buy a new set of irons. I've been playing this game for twenty years and it's been all hand-me-downs and cheapies. After the Wilson woods from Caldor's, I bought a driver—inexplicably called the Balloon System—and it did me just fine until I got somewhat serious about the game. Golf *can* be played on a budget and that's really what I've tried to do. This approach left me with more money for greens fees, that's for sure.

One piece of advice I received—and I know that Dr. Dave heard it, too—is to avoid shelling out for the big-money driver until you can actually hit the big-money driver. Many a man has cut his teeth on a wood made of wood. (Imagine, a wood made of wood . . .) I know that up until last month, the driver that Dr. Dave was hitting looked like something out of Ernie's bag. For you old-school weekend warriors out there, it was a Gene Rosburg handed down from his father.[18]

A Gene Rosburg. This mallet recalls the days of P. G. Wodehouse, he of golf fiction fame. Old school golf clubs had strange, strange names and it was by reading Wodehouse that I learned about them. They are clubs with names that recall the days of Mary, Queen of Scots. Back in the day . . . A niblick was a high-loft iron, like a seven or a nine. A *mashie* was a mid-range iron, most often the five. The aforementioned brassie was a 2-wood

---

[18] *Just like that elephant ass joke!*

and that goofy, gaffy wood of a baffie was a club with some loft: a baffie spoon. Ernie started out with such clubs and so did Dr. Dave, but he no longer carries woods that have names like characters in *Star Wars*. No, no, no. Those days are over 'cuz Dr. Dave went shopping.

Before wielding that credit card, though, he called on two members of our Thundering Herd for advice. Phat Head Andy and ButtNut have a wealth of knowledge. Quiet until called upon, they are sages of the sand traps; buddhas of the bunkers; gurus of the greens. (OK, I'll stop now.) Phat Head is a seven-handicapper and Dr. Dave turned to him first. ButtNut he used for affirmation. And in Dr. Dave's search for new irons, both men suggested Callaways.

Dr. Dave told me, "I was determined to buy used clubs because I don't have the cabbage and I still don't play enough to think about new clubs. Nor do I need the 'cutting edge' for my game."

A few minutes of searching lead Dr. Dave to Callaway's pre-owned website (www.callawaygolfpreowned.com). Callaway has a buy-back program for people who purchase new sets. A perfect barter system for all involved. Dr. Dave found a relatively untarnished set of four-year-old irons—"You won't be able to tell the clubs aren't new" is the claim on the website and Dr. Dave sees no reason to argue—for half the price of a new set, so he got all he needed.[19] Callaway introduces new clubs every two years, so Dr. Dave's set is two models past, but after hitting thirty-year-old irons, he's pretty sure this won't be a problem.

If your interest is not yet piqued, the good doctor reports that these clubs also came with new grips and, even better, a money-back guarantee. Plus, free shipping! It's all a part of Callaway's

---

[19] *A set includes pitching wedge, 9-, 8-, 7-, 6-, 5-, 4-, and 3-irons for a total of eight clubs. You'll probably want to add a sand wedge and, of course, a putter.*

pre-owned certification program, similar to what many car dealers are now offering. The deal was so good that Dr. Dave, despite being the smartest of all The Thundering Herd, was dragged even closer to the precipice of addiction. And go over the edge he did, my friends. The good doctor jumped quite willingly.

The day after he bought the Callaways, he logged onto Golfsmith.com where he unearthed a "limited-time offer" on a cheap-but-modern wood—i.e., graphite shaft and not a bit of wood to be found—a driver called a Lynx Black Cat.[20] Much to Dr. Dave's liking the club, which normally retails for $200, was on sale for $30. New! Of course, there's reason for suspicion, but he was willing to take the $30 risk. Seems to me like a good chance to take!

According to the most up-to-date reports, when last seen Dr. Dave was playing golf on a forty-degree January day, new clubs in tow. He is hoping to shave eight to ten strokes off of his average score this year—he hasn't yet started to record a handicap—while still managing to remember his kids' birthdays, his address, and his wife's name!

In an exuberant e-mail, he closed with an age-old sentiment; confirmation of the depths of his new-found addiction: "Now all I have to do is find the time and the money to play more." Welcome to the world of weekend warrior golf, fella.

When it comes to me and golf gear, I usually avoid the store—and all of those tempting websites—but for once or twice a year. You ever notice how all of these places are either "discount" or a "warehouse" or both? Yet rare is the time that you will find one of these stores in a warehouse. And rarer still are the discounts. But as Dr. Dave can attest, there are deals out there. And

---

[20] *The first graphite shaft was introduced in 1973 and Taylor-Made was the first company to make metal woods.*

so it was, a few weeks back, that I went to check out a new golf store with hope in my heart and a bent hosel in my bag.

When you consistently bang a wood off of the ground like I do, over time the head twists. After the shopkeep Keith took a look at my 3-wood, he estimated that the hosel (head of the club) was turned at a twenty-degree angle. I told him I'd been hitting it that way for more than a year!

In recent months, though, the 3-wood had fallen out of favor. As consistency plummeted like the stock market, I began to warm up to the driver. When my man Egg Head—one of the better golfers in The Thundering Herd—gave me his irons and a 7-wood a couple years back, I bought my first real driver and my first real 3-wood. I went for broke, buying the driver that Tiger was hitting at the time: a Titleist 975D with a 9.5 loft. The shaft is graphite with a stiff flex.[21] The 3-wood I chose was a Callaway Big Bertha Steelhead Plus 3. This was real gear. I was a real man. I was a real man with real clubs with real head covers! I was finally a real golfer!!!

But reality returned and my scores still hovered closer to 100 than 90 and as the summer of 2004 wore on, the Big Bertha was quickly disappearing from my radar screen. I found myself turning to the 4-iron and laying up instead. (I have no 5-wood, although this is for no reason other than basic economics.) More and more I was choosing to let Bertha rot away, her with her bent hosel and me coming up short of the green. Keith handed the wounded war hatchet back and led me to the rear of the store. There, like so many other golf enclaves, was a net and a tee, a smattering of balls, and a computer. I tried six different 3-woods; after every swing, the computer told me about my club speed and

---

[21] *Shaft flexibility comes in "L" for ladies, "A" for seniors, "R" for regular, "S" for stiff, and "X" for extra stiff. The degree of flexibility differs from one club manufacturer to the next.*

the subsequent ball speed, the distance the ball had traveled in the air, and how far offline it was when it landed. Looking at the monitor, I learned about where the point of contact was, on the face of the club, and the loft of the ball as it flew away from me and into the net. The simulator then asked if I wanted to make 'em Biggie Fries and if I'd like paper or plastic. Cash back? I got to vote for the president and even check on my eBay bids!

Dr. Dave and I are equally cheap and so I didn't buy a 3-wood that day, deciding to ride it out for another year or two with my hackneyed hosel. "No point in dropping $80 for reshafting when you can get a new club for $150," said the shopkeep Keith. Of course, he'd had me demo 3-woods in the $200-$250 range, but I can't blame him. The guy had just opened a new business, after all.

I may be a penny-pincher, and my wife may have a degree in common sense (that's *comminus sensicus* in Latin; you can actually see it on her diploma), but I drove home dreaming of a new 3-wood in my hands, the computer tracking the ball as it flew 235 yards, straight like arrow. The screen had even told of forty yards of roll. Beeeeautiful. By the time I turned into my driveway, I had it all rationalized out: it's a write-off, hon. "Hon" being my accountant.

Fortunately, there are folks to turn to in times like these. I immediately sent an e-mail to my gear guru, not Phat Head or ButtNut, but the man who had given me my bag and my irons. A man called Egg Head. And I quote: "Sowe, way too expensive and way too much technology . . . You are so close to finding a solid groove with your swing and when you do, you will be happy in your pants. Take half that amount of money and go to a local course and buy a few lessons. Spend your money on fixing your swing and then treat yourself to a new piece of equipment once you break 90. I'm a big fan of the reward system for golf." Without the swing, equipment does not matter. Thank you, Eggy.

So on that day, it was only knowledge that I took from the shopkeep Keith. Who knew, for example, that irons could be adjusted? I mentioned loft and lie before; I'd never even heard of lie before that day. Loft, of course, is the angle of the face of the club. At one end of the spectrum is my driver, with a loft of 9.5 degrees.[22] At the other is my fifty-six-degree sand wedge. Lie, on the other hand, is the angle of the bottom of the club. For example, Keith could tell that I raise my hands up, ever so slightly, at the point of contact. This, he knew, because the black undercoating of my 3-wood had been worn away (which is how I ended up banging my hosel half way around the shaft). If you haven't beaten your club into the ground, a pro or shopkeep can simply put black tape along the base of the club to determine where it makes contact with the ground (or mat). The loft *and* lie can both be adjusted two degrees if, and only if, the irons are forged. My Tommy Armour 845 irons are not and there you have it.

As they were conceived when Carter was the president, I'm pretty sure that Dr. Dave's irons are also not forged, but he will try to survive another season or two before buying a new set. Unless, of course, that addictive itch returns before the spring . . .

In talking gear, golf clubs are obviously the most important thing, but they aren't the only thing. When it comes to shoes, most public courses don't mind sneakers. It's tough, though, to get proper footing on a wet spring day without spikes. And if you're going to buy golf shoes, buy them with soft spikes. Most clubs have outlawed everything else; they just do too much damage to the course. You ought to be able to get a cheap pair for less than $50 or a decent pair for around $100. If you're going to play five or

---

[22] *The ball stays low unless I tee it high. Windy conditions in Myrtle, for example, forced me to tee closer to the ground in order to keep the ball down.*

more times a year, I'd definitely recommend making some sort of purchase, even if the place you play doesn't require golf shoes.

And speaking of rainy days, pick up a waterproof windbreaker. Golf umbrellas aren't necessarily necessary as there will be plenty of times that your hands are too full—literally and figuratively—to hold an umbrella. The waterproof windbreaker provides the best chance of staying dry. Also, get something to cover up your clubs while they're in the bag. The clubs that drip have the grips that slip and you could definitely kill somebody inadvertently flinging an 8-iron down the fairway. Carry a towel or two, too.

Now, the balls. The gutties. The featheries. The tree sap and rhino mucus! If your average score is consistently over 90, don't kill your wallet with expensive golf balls. Spending approximately one dollar per ball should be just fine. (The Top-Flite XL 3000s I just picked up ran me $16 for fifteen balls.) When you get better, you might want to upgrade to the Callaways or Nikes or Titleists which will run you upwards of thirty dollars a dozen, but not now. You might as well throw five-dollar bills into The Drink!

In your golf bag, you'll want to have a tool for repairing the green (more on that to come) as well as a ball marker for when everyone is on the green. Oftentimes, your golf glove will come with an attached ball marker. Once you lose this—and you will lose it—you can always use a dime. And if the dime or ball mark is in the direct path of someone else's putt, just move it one club head or club length away, at a ninety-degree angle, and then replace after the other putt has gone by. And a little etiquette lesson for those not yet in the know: Whoever is furthest from the hole putts first. If a guy is on the fringe, the playing partner who is about to pull the flag out of the hole may ask, "You want me to tend it?" This means that he won't pull the flag out until the putt is on its way. Usually, this offer is made when the golfer cannot see the hole as he prepares to putt.

Using his green repair tool, Phat Head penetrates and twists, surrounding the hole with three or four of these maneuvers.

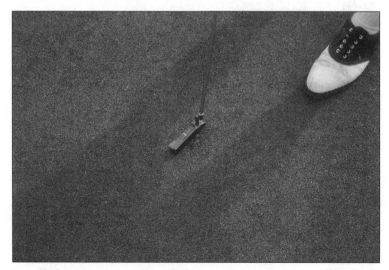

Instead of stepping down with his shoe, Phat Head uses his putter as oftentimes the grass seed from the fairways is different from the grass seed on the greens. For example, at World Tour Golf Links the fairways are Bermuda while the green is bent grass.

I know that this is the gear chapter, but while on the topic of being a good guy on the green, why don't we take Phat Head up on his ecologically correct, etiquette-oriented lesson.

Phat Head cares about course maintenance, having worked in the business for several years out at Vail Golf Course. For him, green repair is a moral responsibility. "Repair for others as you would have others repair for you," Phat Head's golf bible says. Tidying up your ball mark and at least one other is a great way to keep greens in tip-top shape. See below to learn how.

Now, we've got to get off of the green and return to the gear. Three weeks after submitting this manuscript, the better half and I will be flying to Mexico for a wedding and yes, I've signed up for the "Unlimited" golf package at The Mayan Palace! So, this past weekend I began to ready my clubs and bag. Here's what I found when I opened it up for the first time since October.[23]

RANDY'S GOLF BAG

1. Golf clubs: I currently carry fourteen clubs in my bag. First, there is the putter. I have a real love-hate relationship with this Ping Zing 2. It is a hand-me-down from Egg Head and has always seemed just a bit long in the shaft for me. I also carry a Cleveland fifty-six degree sand wedge to go along with my Tommy Armour 845S Oversize, cavity-balanced, steel-shaft irons (pitching wedge through 9-iron). The 7-iron is an eBay replacement and is slightly different from the rest of the set as it is a Silver Scot, rather than an Oversize (when I get my clubs regripped, this club will be the impetus as it is worn smoother than a baby's bum). I have two Big Bertha Steelhead Plus woods (a 7 and a 3) from Callaway

---

[23] *Keeping in mind my twenty-four handicap, I'll understand if you choose not to use my bag as an example!*

and the Titleist driver. The 3-wood has a steel shaft while the hand-me-down 7-wood has a firm graphite shaft (and a head cover that was knitted by Cabbage's grandmother). Someday, all of my clubs will have shafts that are stiff and made of graphite. Someday . . . Also, before moving on, I do carry a beat up old 3-iron for hitting off of rocks and tree roots. I know nothing about it except that its name is El Dorado, written in fancy red script. Fancy.

2. Big pocket in back: Approximately twenty spare balls, a handful of tees, and a spring-loaded toy to make the ball pop back out of the hole after the putt, and a scorecard better lost than found.

3. Main pocket: Fifteen Top-Flite XL 3000 golf balls, twenty-plus tees, two ball markers, one green repair tool, a pencil, and a dime.

4. The smaller, auxiliary pockets: Starting with the top two pockets, I have upwards of two dollars in change, two driving range tokens, a Zippo lighter, a cigar cutter, a cigar band from the best cigar, Cuban or otherwise, that I have ever smoked (a $60 Zino Platinum Chubby Especiale, compliments of Johnny Mac), a half-full bottle of Advil that expired in May of 2004 (I'm thinking I might have to toss that out), *y un peso*. The next two pockets contain a scorecard from my bachelor party, two Band-Aids, a bottle of Coppertone SPF 15, "sweatproof" sunblock, and a bottle of Off. While playing I put my keys, wallet, and cell phone inside. I hate swinging with anything other than tees and a ball or two in my pants pockets.

5. I also have a golf umbrella, despite my earlier advice, in the side sleeve.

6. Attached to the bag is my Amy Mickelson Open bag tag from last year. Two thousand four marked the third annual gathering of The Thundering Herd at my house for golf and

barbecue and the bag tag proudly states this. The Captain made them, complete with a photo of everyone's favorite golf widow, Mrs. Phil Mickelson.[24] I also have two golf towels on my bag, one from the Pete Dye course in the Dominican Republic, Teeth of the Dog, and another from Callaway.

Before getting into the specifics of improving your game, I'd like to spend just a minute or two on the tee, that little wooden prop from which all drives, good and bad, are launched. There are the humongous "step down" tees that look like game pieces and there are the regular ol' 2¼ inchers. And as we all know, everything is big in Texas. That's why the long tees, ranging from 2¾ inches to 3¼ inches in length, are most often referred to as Texas Tees. These are recommended for those oversized drivers, especially with a low loft (anything below ten degrees). They also work well in loose soil when trying to tee up high.

Buy in bulk is the motto, as I usually go with the cheapest tees I can find. Sometimes, I even let superstition come into play and use a tee I've found on the tee box (especially if it's colorful!). And sometimes, on short par 3s, I skip the tee entirely, hitting one of my high irons or wedges right off of the green, green grass of the tee box. Just put some thought into your tee selection and also, put some thought into how deep you sink said tee. Be aware of the weather, especially the aforementioned wind. What we encountered in Myrtle Beach was the last dying breaths of Hurricane Ivan. Make no mistake, though, these were gusts of thirty to fifty miles per hour. Balls destined for greatness went from being pin-seekers to Randy Johnson sliders. Blowing left to right and right

---

[24] *You'll notice the identities of my Thundering Herd have been concealed throughout. This is because The Captain, for example, made our AMO bag tags while at work. The Jimmy plans our Myrtle trips, Egg Head and Dr. Dave shop at Golfsmith.com, and Phat Head checks his fantasy golf stats, all while at work!*

to left was the least of our problems, though. It was the in-your-face and at-your-back wind that made club selection a potshot of a guesser's game. For many of The Thundering Herd, hitting knock-down drives was near impossible. The only chance we stood was to tee down with regulation-sized tees and swing low-loft clubs.

If you don't believe me, check out the sea grass blowing in the wind as The Captain tees off.

6

Shaving Some Strokes

I arrive and wait as some other guy, twice as good as me, is given tips on how to hit a power fade. The two men shake hands like world leaders, promise to play a round together sometime soon, and then brush past me and my clunky clubs without a smile. Apparently, The Pro will acknowledge me when he's good and ready.

After five minutes at the front desk, flirting quite successfully with the check-in girl while picking his teeth with a tee, The Pro saunters my way. Before stepping out into the sun, he verifies my legitimacy with said check-in girl. All signals begrudgingly go, he jams a cigarette into his mouth and then pushes through the door without holding it open for me. He knows I will follow.

"Pro" must be short for prostitute, the only other job in America that allows you to smoke while you work. The smug bastards always look on with casual conceit as I flail away at the ball. Their khakis are always well pressed and their shirts always have exotic logos from exotic locales. They got to go to school in Florida. They were assigned Harvey Penick and Dave Pelz for homework.[25] They know how to hit the ball long and straight and before ten minutes has passed, they will liberate the club from your hands and prove it. Then, like a used condom, they'll hand the club back to you. Postcoital cigarette to follow, of course.

Even if you decide to forgo the lessons, there is much to be learned about your game. There is much work to be done at the driving range. And not just with your driver, either. The nice thing about driving ranges is that these days many of them provide putting greens and even sand traps. And the best part is, to practice putting on different slopes at varying speeds, you don't need to drop a dime. To figure out how much sand to take up, you can leave that wallet in your pocket. Bring a couple of balls from home and have at it. There really is no excuse.

And all kidding aside, if you can swing it (pun intended) I do recommend a session or three with a pro. I'm going to get you started here on the road to Wellville, but like the health advice I'll share shortly, you should seek out a better-informed source if you're in serious trouble. Whether it's a swing doctor or a medical doctor you need, don't hesitate!

---

[25] I carry Penick's Little Red Book and Tommy Armour, Jr.'s Classic Golf Tips in my golf bag.

The following is a highly scientific mélange of information, presented in a multimedia format. By this, I mean we have both photographs *and* illustrations. It's time to think about your grip, to think about your stance, and to think about not thinking about your grip and stance when swinging the club. Also, to think about not thinking about not thinking about your swing while swinging! Look at it this way: it's fine to think about all of these things now, but think of nothing but "straight like arrow" when you swing. Straight like arrow.

ONE BALL, TWO FEET, AND A SHAFT

Let's begin with a mathematical formula, of sorts. Or maybe it's physics I'm thinking of. All I know is you should try to remember the following illustrations when out for your next round. Let rip, see how it feels, adjust, and then try again. Like shooting a basketball, you don't find touch, touch finds you. But also like shooting a basketball, if you don't practice and tinker, tinker and practice, you can't expect touch to ever seek you out. Just remember this: the longer the shaft, the closer the ball should be to your front foot. Conversely, the shorter the shaft (high irons and wedges), the closer the ball should be to your back foot. That's my favorite kind of formula: short and sweet.

When hitting your driver, the ball should sit on the tee parallel to your front foot, give or take an inch. This shot comes on the tee box and nowhere else. Once you hit the fairway, pull out the 3-wood and address the ball so that it's an inch or two back from that front foot. The shaft of the 3-wood is shorter than the driver, so already you're seeing the formula at work!

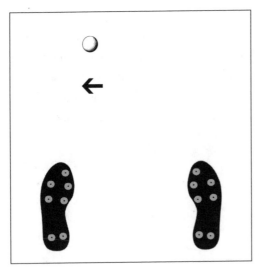

When hitting your 7-wood or 4-iron, the ball should be parallel to the inside of your front knee, four or five inches back from your front foot. Generally, this is a real "go for it" shot, but don't overswing. Let the club do the work for you. With the 7-wood, you'll get some loft. With that 4-iron, you'll be takin' a trip to Line Drive City.

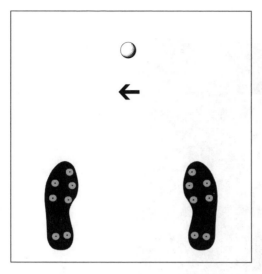

When hitting your 6- or 7-iron, the ball should be right in the middle, in line with your belt buckle. If you're hitting these mid-irons, you're within striking distance, friend. Best of luck!

When hitting your 9-iron or wedges, the ball should be two or three inches forward of your back foot. In turn, you'll want to open up your front foot. Just don't try and force the "touch." You'll send the ball skittering off of your open club face and will end up angrier than you've been in a long, long time.

FOR DISTANCE

Phat Head's grip features the right thumb, slightly forward, and the right pinky hooked (unlike when he putts) behind his left index finger. You can tell he's holding a 4- or 5-iron by looking at the way the shaft is pretty much right in the middle.

The Holgerdude demonstrates where the top thumb shouldn't be. Either straight down the shaft, or, like Phat Head does, slightly forward so as to help fight off the slice. (WARNING: Only a highly-trained trained professional should lie between The Holgerdude's legs while he's swinging his driver. Any club for that matter.)

Phat Head is precise from start to finish, keeping his head over the ball and bending only his left knee and his right arm. His wrists are cocked, too. All things that he works on at the driving range. A good golfer like Phat Head knows how to make mid-round adjustments, too, whereas a golfer like me does not. Waaah.

Ain't nothin' like a Phat Head follow-through. Fear not, this shot didn't turn out like Tin Cup. It was clean and on the green!

And then there's Ish ... He might have a Paul Bunyan swing, but you can't fault the kid for tryin'. For his zippy spikes, neither.

APPROACH SHOTS AND BUNKER BLASTERS

Look at ButtNut pitching up to the green at Wild Wing and all you can say is beautiful fairway, beautiful green, beautiful shot.

It all begins with the setup and The Captain does everything right, including not "grounding" his club (you may not touch the sand with your club before taking your swing). Open stance, quiet legs and relaxed grip; a relaxed back, too, and that's key for an old geezer like The Captain.

The Jimmy stands a chance here as he drags his hands ever so slightly, preparing to hit pay dirt about one inch behind the ball. With a near full-force swing, he scooped it right out of there.

PUTTING

Lesson #1 comes with two simple words: peach basket.

The Holgerdude says, "When a buddy is getting ready to line up a big putt, just set his mind at ease by saying, 'Peach basket.' The person putting should think of the hole as a peach basket. Big and welcome. Fruitful."

Say it with me now, people: "Peach basket!"

Phat Head's putting routine starts with working out the kinks in the condo.

And all that practice pays off as he drains this ten-footer, big break and all! Championship baseball teams always have a reliable closer. Likewise, putting should be yours. You can't close out a hole if you can't putt. . . .

For a few years now, I've kept track of my putts (just beneath my score for the hole).[26] By recording the putts, I've forced myself to concentrate more while on the green. Knowing I'll have to jot it down upon returning to the cart, then add it up upon completing the round, is enough to help me avoid those five or six shoulda/coulda/woulda holes. It helps me shave off a couple inches worth of misses. Most of the time . . .

Nowadays when I go to the driving range, I break the bucket up by spending some time on the putting green. With my bad

---

[26] *5/2 is what my two-putt bogey might look like on a par 4.*

back, it's killer to knock out fifty swings in a half an hour, anyway. So, halfway through, I take a break and pull out the putter.
I get my work in and then hit the sand trap or return to the fun
of boooombs away. Keeping in mind grip and stance and not
thinking about thinking, of course.

*One last reminder on grip:
when swinging, squeeze
with the lead hand and
guide with the rear. Just
imagine yourself opening
a beer. Phat Head's left
hand grips tightly, but the
right hand, his rear hand,
pops the top ever so gen-
tly. Oh blessed swing oil,
nectar of the golfing gods!*

7

How to Get on the Course and Who to Play With

E rnie cherished every hole played with his Thundering Herd and I heard countless stories about guys with nicknames like Smally (he was short) and Shoe (he was once a shoe shine). Although most of his stories included highlights—like those four holes-in-one—I suspect that in Ernie's waning days the quality of play didn't matter as much as the quantity. He knew that he was lucky to have played as much as he did. And to have had the fellas to play with. I know one thing for sure: there are plenty of guys out there who'll drop everything for a round; guys who love their children, their spouses, their dogs, cats, and neighbors, but who really, really *love* their golf.

For those of you who have yet to tap into this local network of club-wielding weekend warriors, might I make a suggestion?

Take the bull by the horns!!! On one of those lazy, early spring, lay-on-the-couch kinds of days, go to the local muni (aka public golf course) and play by yourself. I suggest this time of year, not only for the fact of kicking off the new season, but also because golf leagues are still forming. Ask the guy at the pro shop about leagues. Leave your number and maybe a team will ring you up when they need a substitute. Usually, these leagues go out one day a week, during the week, after work. Many limit play to nine holes, which is perfect for the time-strapped golfer.

Hacker Facts

Teams in league play consist of four players of four different skill levels, based on handicap. They are ranked as A (the best), B, C, and D (the not-so best). Two teams are matched up each week with the two As playing one another, so on and so forth . . .

I realize that leaving your name and number with another man might not come naturally, but if you want this bad enough you'll fight your testosteronic instincts. You'll reach out and if you're lucky, you'll get game.

There are also some options that don't require the gift of gab. For instance, the Internet is the perfect place for you introverts. One problem-solving website is *www.eteeoff.com*. They boast more than ninety courses in my home state of Connecticut and over five hundred in New York, including the site of the four holes-in-one, Mohansic. Sites like this have really grown in popularity in recent years; I've even found tee times available for bid on eBay! Some services you have to pay for, kind of like a subscription, while some just charge a percentage whenever you book through them. In places such as Myrtle, you'll find golf masters who act like travel agents. Golf Master Jim helped us the first time The Thundering Herd stormed into town. He made all of our arrangements, outside of the flights, and his take was nearly invisible when divided amongst twelve guys.

Also, you should know that you *can* make tee times and break them. Most places simply require a few hours notice. At Lyman Orchards, where I play the majority of my rounds, all they ask is two hours. And although they say they will charge for no-shows, I've had a number of buddies bail last minute, especially during big outings like my annual Amy Mickelson Open, but the course has yet to hold me accountable.

Now, back to the virtual reservation and match-making systems of the worldwide web . . . There is also *www.teetimesecretary.com*, which takes care of booking tee times and can even pair you up with other interested players. With all due respect, though, I find finding people to play with to be no problem. If I go by my lonesome, the starter will put me in with a couple of other like-minded folks. I don't mind playing with strangers, especially since by The Turn they're no longer strangers.

Now, let's say you're allergic to computers and don't care to listen to someone's problems over the pretense of golf club camaraderie. Maybe it's worth it to get in seven holes, solo, rather than eighteen with some sloppy joe who thinks it's OK to prattle on about how happy he is that his wife left him (as he cries into his fourteenth beer). Seriously, some of my all-time favorite rounds have been initiated by and attended by me, myself, and I. Rarely do I get to play *all* by myself, but there have been a few times and it's been fantastic.[27] Not only speedy, but very peaceful.

Most of my solo flights have come in the fall as I try to squeeze in as many holes as possible before Jack Frost tees off. The deals for twilight golf tend to be pretty good, especially after Labor Day. Just do what you can. Summer, spring, winter, fall, make the time to play. You don't need no stinkin' formal invitation. You don't have to get involved, like I do, with a lot of hoopla and e-mail banter in the days leading up to the outing. You don't even need to play a full eighteen. Just so long as you're out there. Just so long as you're swingin' 'em.

Allow me a moment to make absolutely clear my love for this game. Allow me one last opportunity to tempt you, if you don't yet consider yourself a weekend warrior hacker, with the apple that is golf . . .

This fall, when The Thundering Herd hit Myrtle, it was for Tuppa's bachelor party. His straits were even more dire than Dr. Dave's, in terms of the golfing gear, as he lives in Africa. So dedicated was I to the task at hand that I lugged two travel bags full of clubs through LaGuardia, one for me and one for Kunta Kinte. And trust me, my fellow weekend warriors, it was worth it. Ten guys out playing five rounds—more fun than any of us deserve. And one back nine stands out, in particular.

---

[27] *I am convinced that when my hole-in-one finally comes, it will be with no one else around. Just! My!! Luck!!!*

Here we are at the first tee for Wild Wing's Hummingbird course. The author is the guy with the smile on his face.

That first day, we played Wild Wing—an exotic bird sanctuary masquerading as three courses. After a rain delay-induced lunch at the nineteenth hole, we were told that no one would be allowed out again. Something about a tornado warning . . . Even so, four Thundering diehards decided to wait it out. The six who quit—I'm embarrassed to say I was among them—found the road home blocked by a fallen tree and so returned, commandeering three carts, clubs in hand and flip-flops on our feet. We got out in time to catch up with Egg Head, Phat Head, The Captain, and Dr. Dave and the course was ours.

Never in my life have I played in a tensome, but as the birds returned to their roosts, we proceeded unmolested. There was Longest Drive and Closest to the Pin and I kid you not, all ten balls found the green. I think it came so easy because we were all feeling so relaxed. Straight shots fell where we'd intended as white-winged birds looked on. The rains stayed away and nary a ranger was to be found although Beverage Girl came by. Twice. It was a beautiful thing.

So, I guess I'm going for broke here. Not only am I telling you to play more golf, I'm telling you to take road trips. If you have the means and you have a Herd, go somewhere and play! And as far as somewhere go, you can't do much better than Myrtle.

TOP FIVE REASONS TO GO TO MYRTLE BEACH FOR GOLF

1. Seven of Myrtle's courses were listed in *Golf Digest's* "100 Greatest Public Golf Courses" article. The Dunes Golf and Beach Club even managed to crack the top twenty! The other six are Barefoot Resort and Golf (the Love Course)— this is our destination next year—King's North at Myrtle Beach National, Tiger's Eye Golf Links, Tidewater Golf Course, True Blue Plantation Golf Course, and Caledonia Golf and Fish Club.

2. Thirty-five of Myrtle's courses earned four stars or better from *Golf Digest.*

3. In addition to more than one hundred golf courses, you will find almost 2,000 restaurants, bars, and nightclubs. Party time.

4. Myrtle Beach golf packages are pretty cheap, as far as vacations go. We do three-day weekends and one thing that makes it even easier are the aforementioned golf masters who will, like travel agents, take care of all of the annoying details.

5. And finally . . . Are you a closet shopaholic? If so, or if you're traveling with someone who is, there's the brand-spankin'-new Mall of the Carolinas. There is also fun to be had, shopping and restaurant-wise, at Broadway at the Beach and Barefoot Landing.

I'm not even on the payroll, folks. I just love it down there. It doesn't get any better than the buildup to a weekend away with my boys. Except for the weekend itself!

After the rain-infused fun of Wild Wing, we hit the ultimate destination—the most entertaining of the ten courses I've played down there. Featuring twenty-seven of the world's greatest holes, World Tour Golf Links was selected by the National Golf Course Owner's Association as the "2004 National Golf Course of the Year." World Tour's holes come from twenty-three different courses in six different countries and ten different American states. Did we find that it lived up to all the hype? I think that the photo tells it all.

Golf Master Jim's cut . . . $25. Plane ticket . . . $200. A round at World Tour . . . $75. Golf balls to replace those lost in the drink . . . $15. Sitting with your boys at TPC Sawgrass's number Seventeen . . . priceless!

You know, we may not have the gumption of the original Thundering Herd, but there was love in South Carolina that weekend. Good ol'-fashioned man love. Not the kind banned by Bush, but the kind that has forged friendships since Adam first left The Garden to meet Stifler at the driving range. And if this line of reasoning isn't convincing enough, if my tales of Myrtle aren't your cup of tea, if the photos don't get your blood pumping, might I recommend *Scrapbooking for Weekend Warriors?*

But let's say you are Mohammed and you just can't go to the mountain. Well then, let's get that mountain to come to Mohammed! Arrange an outing and have your version of The Thundering Herd gather at your place. Their families, too. You'll have to scramble to make the tee times, and do the majority of shopping and cleaning up, but my annual Amy Mickelson Open always leaves me and my boys smiling. The ladies spend the day at the beach with the kids while we hack our way around Lyman Orchards. Then, back home for a joyous reunion and some serious barbecuing. This has actually become a Father's Day tradition, late June being the perfect time for everyone to get together, make some new stories, and retell a bunch of the old. You could throw an AMO of your own, Mohammed.

8

"I Swear, There Are Nineteen Holes in Golf!"

When a buddy tells you about losing money at the casino, add a hundred bucks to the total. If he says he lost "only" $225, that means he lost $325. By the same token, wise guys sometimes *minimize* their gains. "I won, but only $65" is merely an attempt to get out of picking up the tab at the diner. Don't fall for it. Your boy really won $165, so take him for all he's worth: milkshakes, burgers, cheese fries, and all!

There's a lesson to be learned here. And nothing to do with gambling, either. At least not directly.

The Exaggeration Theory, when properly applied, can help enhance your golfing experience. For example, think in terms of hours rather than dollars. And think larger (and longer) rather than smaller. What I'm getting at is this: your average weekend round on your average public course will take nearly six hours.

But if you're smart you'll tell the folks at home that you'll be back in seven. This way, you're covered for nineteen holes rather than a mere eighteen.

Every golf course should have a nineteenth hole where, from left to right, bachelor parties (Tuppa), birthdays (Phat Head), and birdies (Egg Head) can be celebrated. You'll note The Ryder Cup on the big-screen TV and the hole-in-one plaques in the background.

Like any lengthy endeavor, the round needs to be rehashed, scores calculated, money change hands. And what better way than over beers in the clubhouse? In order to protect this sacred time, you must build it into the schedule from the get-go.[28] Truth be told, my better half is actually very good about all of this man stuff. In general, The Thundering Herd got pretty lucky in the lady department. (Those who did not . . . well, they didn't quite

---

[28] *The one caveat being if the total time may preclude you from being allowed to play. If that's the case, tell a little white lie in the other direction: "No, it won't take any more than four hours . . ." Real wise, like the guy who underreports his winnings at the casino.*

make it down to Myrtle!) Some days, Alicia does her woman things and I watch the fort. Other days, she does the watching. Come July, baby number two will be upon us and I'm thinking s/he won't do much for my handicap. But I know that Alicia, much as myself, wants to maintain a bit of her non-mother, non-wife, non-worker bee identity. That being said, if the going gets rough, I do have a few tricks up my sleeve. For those of you struggling against the chains of domesticity, a little white lie may be just what the doctor ordered . . .

THE "I SWEAR, IT'S GOOD FOR ME!" LIST OF EXCUSES

1. "The walking, the fresh air, the vitamin C in a cigar . . . A round of golf, it does the body good."
2. "I'm only a couple of rounds away from having a body like Tiger." (Phil Mickelson taught me this one.)
3. "Four out of five dentists surveyed agree: chewing on a tee helps in the fight against gum disease."
4. "Golfers are the smartest guys ever. You know, like doctors and lawyers and stuff? So, the more I play, the smarter I'm gonna be!"
5. "I've been thinking about getting a sex change lately, hon. What could I do to get back in touch with my manly side?"

And if the subtle stuff doesn't work (sex change? subtle?!), you might need to employ one of the following. Good luck, fella.

THE "I SWEAR, IF YOU DON'T LET ME PLAY . . ." LIST OF THREATS

1. "Either you let me play golf or I'm gonna follow you around the house all day, singing stadium anthems. 'We will! We will!! Rock you!!!'"

2. "If I can't get six hours of Me Time, I'm going to stop shaving. And showering. And clipping my toenails!"

3. "When I'm depressed I eat and if I don't go play I'm going to be really, really depressed and I'm going to really eat a lot and I'm going to get really, really fat. Really."

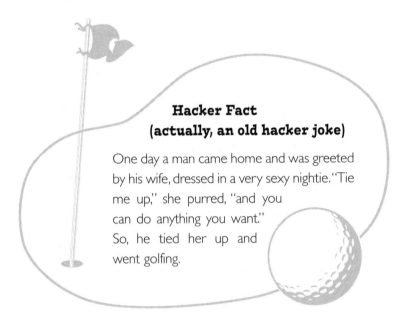

**Hacker Fact
(actually, an old hacker joke)**

One day a man came home and was greeted by his wife, dressed in a very sexy nightie. "Tie me up," she purred, "and you can do anything you want." So, he tied her up and went golfing.

If I haven't yet made clear the depths of my dependence, I guess I'll have to come clean in a more direct manner . . .

Hello. My name is Randy and I'm a golfaholic.

Although inner peace—at least a non-golfer's version of inner peace—continues to elude me, I thought I'd throw a rope to those still hoping to save their wives from golf widowhood. Admittedly, admitting your obsession is the first step to recovery, but recognizing my weakness has yet to change me. And for this, I'm thankful! Still, if you feel like you're drowning in a sea of tee times, like your wife may leave you and your dog might run away as well, well then this twelve-step program may be of help.

THE TWELVE STEPS TO ADMITTING YOUR GOLF ADDICTION

1. I admitted I was powerless over Golf, that my approach— from club selection to shot selection—my attitude, and my handicap had become unmanageable.
2. I came to believe that a Power greater than me could restore me to my youth.
3. I made a decision to turn my life over to the care of Golf *as I understood it.*
4. I made a searching and fearless moral inventory of myself, especially in the area of my short game.
5. I admitted to Golf, to myself, and to another human being the exact nature of my addiction to the game. (You, fellow weekend warrior, are that human being. And for this, I thank you.)
6. I was entirely ready to have Golf remove all these defects of character.
7. I humbly asked The Pro to remove my shortcomings. At a reasonable rate.
8. I made a list of all persons I had harmed with errant tee shots and chili-dip chips and became willing to make amends to them all.
9. I made direct amends to such people wherever possible, except when to do so would injure them or others (example: while they are putting on the next green over) or have a negative impact on my score.
10. I continued to take personal inventory of my balls and whenever I touched the balls of another, promptly admitted it. If I

stepped in someone else's line or talked during their back-swing, as well.

11. I sought thorough lessons and meditation to improve my conscious contact with Golf *as I understood it,* playing only for knowledge of the game and the power to lower my handicap.

12. Having had a spiritual awakening as the result of these steps, I tried to carry this message to other hackers, and to practice these principles in all of my affairs, golfing and otherwise.

Now, if only we could be out playing we wouldn't have all this time to consider addiction and steps and telling white lies!!!

9

Good Golf, Good Eats, and Good Health

When it comes to back spasms, I can certainly sympathize. The Captain, The Holgerdude, and Phat Head Andy, too. Phat Head's problem isn't overly problematic: he simply feels the strain of some extra weight up front. (The existence of a gut hasn't done much to help my cause, either!) Like softball, golf doesn't require a fantastic physique, but you really can't be a fat bastard and expect to play well. Phil Mickelson's body type? Fine. Craig Stadler?[29] Now you're pushing it!

If you're way out of shape and way overweight, be warned. You're liable to be pooped soon after The Turn and, even worse, you're risking death before nirvana, nirvana being that pinnacle

---

[29] *ESPN reports that The Walrus is 5'10" and weighs . . . 240!*

of golf success, the hacker Holy Grail: shooting your age. What can you do? Well, for one, you can walk when you play. Walk every other round and walk every time you go out on your own. Save the cart for the social outings.

Brent Kelley, in *Your Guide to Golf*, writes that, "Walking a golf course is good for your health, good for the course's health, and good for the game's health."

David Fay of the USGA says, "We strongly believe that walking is the most enjoyable way to play golf and that the use of carts is detrimental to the game. This negative trend needs to be stopped now before it becomes accepted that riding in a cart is the way to play golf."

Hacker Facts

The golf cart was invented during the 1930s, but R. J. Jackson held the first golf cart patent, calling his 1948 creation "The Arthritis Special." Today, there are over one million golf carts in the U.S.

Two studies cited at *www.walkinggolf.com* describe, in depth, the health benefits of a round of golf walked. One researcher, Sweden's Gi Magnusson, figured out that four hours of walking is equivalent to "a forty-five-minute fitness class." The second study found that hoofin' it can help to lower bad cholesterol. Now this is advice that I'd be wise to follow. Despite a daily regimen of ten milligrams of Lipitor, I'm still a cigar-smoking, cart-riding, hot dog and hamburger-eating (with cheese, please) hacker. The only good thing about my heart attack habits is that they qualified me to write this book! I admit though, even if these scientists might not be able to putt their way out of a paper bag, they do know their stuff when it comes to good golf and good health. Their advice—and mine—should be heeded.

If you're too out of shape to walk the whole kit 'n' caboodle, find a few opportunities to walk during the round. Let your partner take the cart to look for his ball while you walk up to yours. If you have a 112-yard approach shot from the middle of the fairway, take your wedges and your putter and storm the green after planting the ball within three feet of the pin. Yahtzee! You might also have to find excuses to walk because many courses require carts on the weekends (in the interest of speedy play). Fortunately, most playing partners are more than happy to have the cart to themselves, so whether you're fat, playing on the weekend, or both, there ought to be more than enough opportunity for you to get the lead out.

Now, if you have a bad back like me and a few of my fellow Herdsters, you probably want a pull cart when you walk. Even better is a bag with a double shoulder strap. Single straps are hell on the back and shoulders.

And I wasn't kidding when I said that the experts think that carts are bad for the course. This is especially true after rain—that's why even ninety-degree rules are suspended in lieu of "cart paths only."[30] When carts first came on the scene, Kelley writes, fairways were not as agronomically correct as they are today. They were hard as pavement so the wheels and the weight of the cart did no

---

[30] *The ninety-degree rule means that you can only drive out onto the fairway at a ninety-degree angle, returning at the same, thus minimizing damage.*

damage. Kind of like public courses in late August, burnt-out grass the color of cement. Improvements in turf management mean courses are in better shape than ever. The downside is that wear and tear takes a greater toll. See, not only do I want *you* to be in good shape, I'm looking out for our friend the fairway, as well.

I like my beers, but Brent Kelley makes another good point: carts are conducive to drinking and yapping. The more you drink and yap, the less you think about your next shot. If you're walking, you may be more tired as you approach Eighteen, buuuut you will put more thought into each shot. As you walk, you'll plan. I know that I like to "walk it off" after a bad shot. Taking a little stroll gives me time to calm down and I prefer to live life as calmly as possible. I may have high cholesterol, but I have low blood pressure. If golf makes you angry and sends your blood pressure shooting through the roof, then it ain't so good for you. Try walking it off.

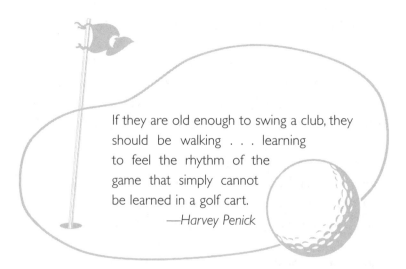

If they are old enough to swing a club, they should be walking . . . learning to feel the rhythm of the game that simply cannot be learned in a golf cart.
—Harvey Penick

In golf, your body warms up as you play. And warming up is a good thing. Some stretching, mixed in with some calisthenics, will increase the temperature of your muscles so that they can contract and relax more quickly.[31] It also raises, gradually rather than traumatically, the heart rate, loosens the connective tissue, and triggers the release of fluid, which promotes the smooth movement of bone over bone.

A good golf swing is an arc of beauty, smooth from start to finish. If your bones are grinding and your connective tissue is tight . . . foooogetaboutit! Knowing this, Phat Head hits the driving range before hitting the first tee. And before hitting the range, he stretches that back. Being the wise old boy that he is, Phat Head is also willing to stretch again during the round. Every break in the action is an opportunity. To crack open a beer or crack your back: both serve to loosen you up. Here now is Phat Head's stretching routine.

Phat Head arranges his clubs then casually stretches his upper half as he scouts out the driving range at Lyman Orchards.

---

[31] *I'm willing to concede on calisthenics. I really don't expect to see you doing jumping jacks at the first tee! But do some stretching. Seriously.*

Phat Head preps his lower back for the day's first swing by swinging his shoulders and twisting at the waist. And you'll notice how he does so without ever having to get down on the ground. Easy as pie. Mmmm, Lyman Orchards makes a nice apple pie . . .

Phat Head needed some help straightening up again from this stretch, but back spasms rarely lead to birdies.

At most courses, there will be a back-up at the first par 3. Take this opportunity, as Phat Head did, to further loosen up.

Forget to stretch before and you're destined to throw that back out. You know when you've done it, too. You know right then and there that you're going to be out of commission for weeks and that everybody at the office is going to look at you funny the next day. When you get home, the better half will smirk and your children will show no mercy. They still want to be picked up and, even worse, chased. Your mother will scold you, your grandmother will call you an idiot, your mother-in-law will give your wife that I-told-you-so look and all because you couldn't take a minute to stretch.

In their book, *Take Care of Yourself*, Donald Vickery and James Fries make some recommendations and I couldn't agree with them more. For one, they suggest having your blood pressure checked every year. Make sure the ol' ticker doesn't rev too high when traversing a hill in pursuit of a lost ball. It's also important that your heart be able to return to resting rate quickly. How else are you going to sink the birdie putt?! For more on this, talk to someone who didn't get a 67 in biology and who has a couple of diplomas on the wall. Written in Latin and not in crayon.

Speaking of the heart and Lipitor, this just in: good cholesterol is good while bad cholesterol is . . . bad! So, even though Vickery and French Fries recommend getting your cholesterol tested every five years, I'm going to err on the side of caution and suggest you go every year. This is especially important if you 1) have an unusually high level of bad cholesterol, 2) have a family history of high cholesterol and/or heart attacks, and 3) are a legend amongst your Thundering Herd for once eating an entire blooming onion all by yourself.

Misters French Fries and Vickery both know that you can't hit a golf ball—let alone track it to its final resting place—if you can't see it. Therefore, they also recommend getting tested for glaucoma. I'm only thirty-three and my doctor is sending me to see the eye doctor. Doc Epstein may be overly cautious, but I'll take it. I'm no biologist, but I know one thing . . . it's very hard to follow a hard-slicing drive into the woods without the benefit of sight. I also know it's impossible to shave three strokes off of the handicap from six feet under. So let's heed the doctor's advice, shall we?

That being said, when it comes to what you should and should not eat, fear not my cookie-loving friends!

"Carbs are to your body what gas is to a car," writes Susan Kleiner in her book *High-Performance Nutrition*. "The major role of carbohydrates in nutrition is to provide energy. During exercise, carbohydrates are one of your main sources of energy."

There are carbs and then there are calories. Everybody agrees, controlling your caloric intake is a pretty good idea. To be specific, it's important to remember that as you age your metabolic rate slows down, which means you will not burn calories as quickly as you once did. We run like rabbits as kids. We trudge like turtles as adults. Obesity is a real threat and being overweight often leads to heart disease, high blood pressure, diabetes, and other badass life-threatening problems. Diabetes is now one of the leading causes of death in the U.S. As we get older, our bodies lose the ability to regulate glucose and this can lead to adult onset, or Type II, diabetes.

Lest you find all this talk too serious, know that many a golfer eats well, even while playing. For example, look at how happy this snack shack sign makes Phat Head![32]

---

[32] *On par 3s, I let Phat Head shoot first and play off of his club selection. I take the same approach at the snack shack. The man has the intuition of a gourmet and the swing of a PGA money leader.*

Eating food that is high in saturated fats and neglecting to exercise are surefire ways to guarantee high cholesterol, especially LDL, otherwise known as "bad cholesterol." This leads to clogged arteries and clogged arteries lead to heart attacks and heart attacks lead to death and death leads to no more trips to Myrtle Beach. Capisce?

Also, think fiber. Not only will eating foods rich in fiber make you regular (yee ha!), it will help fend off the plague. All right, not the plague, but the following list of no-no's are best kept at bay with a healthy, fiber-rich diet: appendicitis, cardiovascular disease, colorectal cancer, constipation (ugh), cavities and gum disease, kidney stones and gallstones, hemorrhoids (oy), hernias, high blood pressure, erectile dysfunction (¡ay caramba!), high cholesterol, heart disease, and ulcers (say goodbye to hot sauce).

EAT THIS STUFF SO THAT YOU CAN HAVE THE OCCASIONAL ONION RING (AND STAY REGULAR!!!)

- Bananas, apples, oranges, strawberries, peaches, apricots, prunes, and pears
- Carrots, peas, canned corn, broccoli, and tomato sauce
- Wheat bread, bran muffins, saltines, graham crackers, granola bars, raisin bran, Fig Newtons, and oatmeal
- Cranberry, apple, orange juice, maple syrup, low-fat milk, and yogurt
- Rice and baked potatoes
- Baked beans, kidney beans, black beans, and lentils
- Mac and cheese and pizza (yes, pizza!)

On a different but related note, the vitamin and mineral supplement business has grown now to sales of more than $3 billion per year. But guess what? If you eat healthy and live an active life, most of these supplements are unnecessary. When you eat decently, you get vitamins. That being said, adults, especially men, can use a daily dose of antioxidants. Vitamin C (citrus fruits, berries, and green leafy veggies), vitamin E (nuts and seeds) and beta-carotene (carrots, sweet potatoes, spinach, broccoli, and fruit)—all considered antioxidants—can reduce risk of cancer and heart disease. They also reduce the risk of tissue damage, which will help keep you active. The less you weigh, the less strain on your body.

The most widely used formula for identifying whether or not you are obese is the Body Mass Index. Grab a calculator and check out the formula below.

$$\left(\frac{\text{Weight}}{\text{Height x Height}} \right) \times 703 = \text{BMI}$$

A score of 18.5–24.9 = Normal
A score of 25–29.9 = Overweight
And a score of 30 and above = Obese
NOTE: *Use inches when calculating height.*

This formula, provided by the folks at the Center for Disease Control (CDC), informed me that I'm a member of the Overweight Club and that if I'm not careful, I might never again have the chance to be careful, let alone the chance to score my first-ever hole-in-one.

The CDC website states: "All persons who are obese or overweight should try not to gain additional weight . . . Whatever your BMI, talk to your doctor to see if you are at an increased risk for disease and if you should lose weight. Even a small weight loss (just 10 percent of your current weight) may help to lower the risk of disease."

Ten percent of 213 pounds is twenty-one pounds. Who're they kidding? That might happen . . . if I had a leg amputated! Still, I'm glad they're looking out for me. For all of us.

Everything I've read says to form good habits at a young age. The problem is, at a young age none of us wants to listen to anything old people have to say. By the time we see the wisdom of their ways, we're amongst them! But I look at it this way: an old dog can be taught new tricks. This is true in all categories, from putting to betting to healthy habits.

Doctors, nutritionists, advice columnists, and Misters French Fries and Vickery all agree: live life enthusiastically. Be actively engaged. Don't let the years, let alone the ass-kicking that is full-time employment, home ownership, and parenthood, slow you down. Make sure to make time for yourself. And be passionate about the things you do. There's nothing wrong with an increased heart rate when the excitement is directed towards positive, productive activity. When you wake up in the morning, you ought to be able to hop out of bed with your heart racing in anticipation. There should be at least one thing that puts a smile on your face; something that even if you don't do it well, you do it with chutzpah. Something like golf.

10

Games within the Game: From the Sword to the Pin

Oh blessed sword, unsheathed for moments of masculinity. Excalibur, ExCallaway, Excellence, Par Excellence. A sword, handed down to Cabbage by two generations of MacGilpin men. Yes, I means what I says and I says what I means. The Thundering Herd is armed and dangerous. We've got a sword!

When my main man Cabbage comes out to play, he has two special treats in his bag: an orange Fisher-Price putter for finishing up on Eighteen (no matter how long the putt and no matter how much is riding on it) and the aforementioned sword. When we hold a Longest Drive contest, the first foursome carries this monument to manliness in one of their carts, spiking it into the ground to mark the first drive.[33] If someone in the second foursome

---

[33] *In order to win Longest Drive, your tee shot must be on the fairway. No fringe. No foliage. Fairway.*

manages to go bigger, longer, better, stronger, they get to pull the sword from the ground ("Excaaaaaalibur!!!") and drive it back in further on down the fairway. I'm telling you, there's nothing more satisfying than doing this. Pure adrenaline! Pure machismo!! You are the biggest and the best, friend. Be unsheathed and stay unsheathed!!!

Although it's nice to have everybody hand you $5, the thing that leaves the winner smiling is knowing, simply knowing, that he is *mas macho* than everybody else in his Thundering Herd. No one will haze him for leaving a putt short or chili-dipping an approach shot into the woods. Not after establishing himself as the King of the Jungle. Not while armed with a sword.

Clearly, if it wasn't for fun like this, if it wasn't for the male ego, if it wasn't for the fact that the most expensive club in my bag is that big-headed Titleist, I'd be a good golfer. But until I get over my need to control the sword—please hold all phallic jokes, no matter how true they may be—I guess I'll continue to be Sir Slice-A-Lot off of the tee. Happy Gilmore when luck is on my side.

I like Longest Drive, but nothing beats the dynamics of trying to best the rest on a par 3. When you get right down to it, there isn't a tremendous amount of pressure-for-precision with the "grip and rip" of the Longest Drive. You're stepping up to the tee with a 3-0 count and a green light from the third-base coach. If you whiff, who cares? If you slice, you lose the contest but your score can be saved with a mulligan. But when lining up with my 8-iron, glory a mere 150 yards away, I have a tendency to get in my own way. I can't help but think about that last par 3, four holes before. You know the one I'm talking about, the one I recorded a six on? The one where I shanked my tee shot, lost the ball, hit my drop thin, chipped up within six inches of the hole, and then two-putted? Yeah, that one. Still fresh in my mind. Still haunting me as I try to win some money and maybe record myself a two.

On this Closest to the Pin, ButtNut has decided to go for it, pulling out a wood to combat the wind and doing his best to not think about the water or that monster trap.

Club selection is key on par 3s and never more so than during a Closest to the Pin contest.[34] You will find golfers honoring the "your honor" system like on no other hole, trying to glean any information they can from the guinea pig of a golfer who hits first.

The way we do our Closest to the Pin is as follows:

1. Although an impromptu Closest to the Pin may break out on a par 4 or 5 fairway (when a couple of golfers find their balls side by side), as a contest we only do it from the tee box on a par 3.
2. You must be on the green to win, no fringe.
3. In theory, it's a $1 bet, but it never plays out that way because if the golfer who's closest can birdie the hole, he gets $3 from the other three. If he two-putts for par, he only gets $2. And

---

[34] *A Closest to the Pin contest is also commonly referred to as a Greeny.*

nightmare of all nightmares, if he has to settle for a bogey (or worse), out comes *his* wallet. From hero to goat, go to jail, pass go, do not collect $200. He has to pay the other three guys $1 each for poor putting. Insult to injury.

4. There is also an add-on if you like to reward a nice recovery. A "sandy" is when someone gets up and down out of a sand trap to save par. In that case, the other three pay the savvy sander $1 each.

Oftentimes, Closest to the Pin contests are conducted as a fundraiser. Many courses will agree to let organizations like leper colonies and mascot rehabilitation centers set up shop and for your $10 donation you can win something like a cruise, if and only IF you score one of those ever-elusive, Ernie-inspired holes-in-one. Land on the green without sinking it and there's a consolation prize—usually a golf towel, T-shirt, or sleeve of balls. Send your tee shot into the drink and the philanthropist will wish you well, thank you for your donation, and call out something clever like, "Enjoy your swim." Down in Myrtle, one such charitable chiquita joked about the lost cruise when Ish took a dip. As his ball was skipping across the pond, she quipped, "Well, there's *your* cruise." He failed to see the humor.

At the heart of so many of the Games within the Game is money. Not only is there a lot of betting in golf, there's plenty of opportunity for side action.[35] When proposing or accepting a bet, nobody thinks about this: every outcome produces a winner, but also a LOSER. And the world is full of losers looking to make back some of their money. Thus the need for side action.

When a bettor loses a bet, when things just don't pan out the way he envisioned before phoning his bookie, shaking hands with

---

[35] *Side action is a bet on top of a bet—oh, how I love human innovation!*

his buddy, mouthing off to the guy down the bar, or sinking that first tee into the supple soil, well then there's only one thing to do . . . hope that someone will give you the chance to bet again! Fortunately, courses are full of guys more than willing to take more of your money. When a golfer offers a press, it's a kindness extended: essentially a side-action deal of double or nothing. And no matter how poorly you've been playing, the press must be accepted. To turn down a press is to admit that you are impotent, have always been impotent, and that your children are not your own. To turn down a press is to raise a banner that says, "I AM WORTHLESS AND WEAK!" Or, if you don't have that much paper and paint, "I SUCK!!!" To run from the opportunity to erase your debt is to say that you have absolutely no confidence in your game. It is to admit that you need what little money is left in your wallet to pay for your Viagra prescription.

The press is most often used as part of the ever-popular Nassau bet. If you want to learn about all sorts of golf betting games, I recommend *Chi Chi's Golf Games You Gotta Play* from everybody's favorite old-school golfer, Chi Chi Rodriguez. I would love to sit and talk golf with the man; share a pitcher of sangria and hear all about his eight PGA victories and about how close he came to realizing every golfer's dream when he finished within one shot of shooting his age (he scored a 67) at the 2002 Bruno's Memorial Classic. Afterwards, I could tell him all about Cabbage's sword!

The closest I got to Chi Chi, unfortunately, was reading his take on the Nassau bet. "A Nassau is really three wagers in one." One pairing plays against another pairing (otherwise known as match play), where the best score on each hole is used for a team win. One bet is placed on the team score for the front nine, the second bet is placed on the score for the back nine, and the third bet is for the overall round. The dollar value is the same for all three bets and is usually established on the first tee box. A $5 Nassau means $5 to the winner of the front nine, $5 to the winner of the back, and $5 to the overall winner of the match.

NASSAU BETS AND HOW THEY'RE SCORED

- Team A wins the front nine holes "3 and 2" (an insurmountable three-hole lead, with two holes to play) and so each player wins $5.
- Team B wins the back nine holes "1 up," which means they win the final hole—the eighteenth—to break a tie.
- Team A still wins the third bet, the overall bet, "2 and 1" (an insurmountable two-hole lead, with one hole—again, the eighteenth—to play.

NOTE: *If the guy you're playing against says you're "all square," he isn't calling you a dork. All square means the score is tied!*

Another fun, less-complicated competition is called skins. If you've never played or seen it, tune in to ABC during Thanksgiving weekend and check out "The Skins Game." To win a hole in a skins game, one must have the lowest score. If there's a tie, the hole carries over so that the next is worth two skins. And the best part, as far as us betting hackers and hacking bettors are concerned, is that the possibilities are endless. Different holes are assigned different dollar values, based on their difficulty, and to keep everyone involved, the dollar values are increased for the last few holes. Just think of the high stakes fun of Texas Hold'em with the physical demands of an athletic competition. It doesn't get much better than that!

The shoot-out offers a similar kind of high-pressure, go-for-it, Game within the Game kind of fun. This is an elimination game based on the match play format in which one player gets dropped after each hole (based on having the highest score for that hole). If two golfers have the high score, no one gets the boot till the next hole. This is sudden death, balls-to-the-wall stuff and should not be confused with "The Franklin Templeton Shootout," Greg Norman's charity event to benefit CureSearch National Childhood Cancer Foundation.

Now, a game to return us to kinder, gentler times. . . . Yes, friends, it's Animal Cards (some people call this game Wolf). There are four cards, none of which you want in your possession at round's end. The cards are actually bag tags and if, for example, you lose a ball or hit it out of bounds, you are given the Gorilla card to attach to your bag. Following the rules of Hot Potato, you need to hope somebody else goes out of bounds before holing out on Eighteen. The Frog card is given to the first player to get wet. As soon as somebody else plops down in a water hazard, he's passed the Frog card to attach to his bag. Majority rules when there is a debate over just how wet wet is. The Camel card goes to the first player to land in the sand. Be it a waste bunker, a fairway trap, or one of those annoying bunkers guarding the green, the Camel is yours! Finally, there's the Snake card. You're given this if and when you three-putt. Or four-putt. Or worse. Attach that Snake card to your bag and start wishing awful things upon your friends the next time you're all on the green.

And let me take this opportunity to remind weekend warrior golfers everywhere that when a buddy says, "That's a gimme," you still have to add an additional stroke to your score for the hole. Your boy is just giving you a free pass on the final putt.[36] If he offers this after your fourth stroke, you've got to take a five. I've seriously played with guys who forget to add that final stroke. I mention it here because if that gimme means your *third* putt is assumed, then the Snake card is yours. No ifs, ands, or buts.

It's up to the group what the losers will owe, but I like the idea of the Frog buying the first round, the Snake paying the tip, the Gorilla buying the low scorer a sleeve of balls (symbolic, don't you think?), and the Camel stuck with arranging the next outing, even if he has to bust hump to secure the tee times.[37]

Somewhere between a "Game within the Game" and a "Variation of the Game We Love" is the beloved outing. I say beloved because, more often than not, outings are as much about the golf as they are about socializing. And if it's a company outing, they're free! One time-saver when invading a course in the style of Genghis Khan and his Thundering Herd is the shotgun start. Rather than everybody starting off at the first hole, each foursome is assigned to tee off at a different hole. To state the obvious, if your group is assigned to Fifteen, the eighteenth and final hole of your round will actually be Fourteen. The shotgun start is an especially useful tool for outings because everybody wants to get the most they can out of the nineteenth hole after all is said and done and recorded in the books for posterity. If the company is shelling out for catering, do you want to be the last foursome to tee off? The last to arrive for the post-party? No way. Nobody wants to have to pick through the unwanted runts of the shrimp cocktail platter. No thirsty golfer wants the dregs of the keg.

---

[36] *Usually, if you are "within the leather" (i.e., the length of the grip on your putter), you will be given a gimme. Unless, of course, there's a lot riding on the putt or you've refused to extend this courtesy on earlier holes.*

[37] *Camel puns. Guaranteed to bring the house down every time.*

A nice little time-saving tool called the scramble is often used at outings. (Another name for this is best ball.) Simply put, it's another format designed to give the hackers a break. Yippee! The genius of the scramble is that the foursome is a team and they are allowed to pick which of the four drives they will use to play from for the second shot. Everybody brings their ball up to, assumedly, the longest drive and then hits again. (The exception being a shorter drive in a better spot.) In this way, the team with the best golfer still has a better chance of winning. He will hit the straightest drives, hit the most Greens in Regulation, finish the day with the most one-putts, tell the funniest joke, dazzle all the ladies with his Dockers, tip the most generously, so on and so forth.

(But really, I bear no ill will towards good golfers. Pros, neither. Really.)

The Pope of Slope, whom you may remember from Chapter 2, writes that the concept of the scramble "is based on the individual components of playing a hole—driving ability, approach shot ability, and getting up and down, which includes chipping, bunker play, and putting." Sounds like my Must Improve list . . .

Whether it's you, your employer, or the local fire department doing the organizing, outings are a blast. There's the format of play, the nineteenth hole afterwards, and, more likely than not, some Closest to the Pin and Longest Drive in between. Outside of Ed McMahon showing up at my door with a $10,000,000 check, I can think of no better way to spend the day!

11

Variations of the Game We Love

I do like animals, especially when I'm trying to hit a golf ball through the triple threat of their hind legs and tail. No, I'm not talking about golfing at the circus or zoo. I'm talkin' mini golf!

Although some enthusiasts will go so far as to call miniature golf a sport, I choose to stop short of that claim. I will say this, though: in my opinion, mini golf is *the* greatest vacation game ever invented. What could be better than an hour of mini golf on a warm summer evening, especially if it comes between dinner and the ice cream stand. I don't even care if I played real golf that day. Give me eighteen holes, a purple ball, and the chance to shoot for the clown's nose!

In the early twentieth century, miniature golf quickly gained recognition for being as its name suggests: a miniature version of regulation golf. The recreational pastime hasn't always gone by that name, though. Mini golf has also been referred to as Garden Golf (played on real grass), Tom Thumb Golf (after the first mini golf company to make use of obstacles), Half-Pint Golf (good clean fun for Mom and Dad's little half-pints), Rinkiedink Golf (although it has nothing to do with the name, the theme was setting up a course wherever, whenever, however), and Putt-Putt (after a chain of mini golf franchises that sprang up in the 1950s). Originally, the putting surface was made of pressed cottonseed hulls. Over the past hundred years, many efforts have been made to improve the playing surface. Clay and hard sand have been combined, augmented by green dye called "Grassit." As time went by, course owners moved on to indoor/outdoor carpeting and even Astroturf.

I'm not the only one who likes playing at night. So, back in the day, many a mini golf course was built under illuminated billboards. Some places would stay open as late as 4:00 AM. In the age of Prohibition, though, many towns enacted night ordinances to close the brightly lit courses earlier than that, so as to discourage drinking. I'll admit, sneaking beers onto the course is still kind of fun. More than two, though, and you stand no chance of putting one in the clown's nose!

In the 1980s, hundreds of miniature golf course owners followed Disney's lead, turning their courses into virtual amusement parks. A boom took place in that favorite golfing haven of mine, Myrtle Beach, as pirate ships, mountains, and just about any obstacle you can think of sprouted up from the sandy soil. Without a doubt, Myrtle is the golfing capital of the country—regulation and mini golf alike.

In the 1990s, family entertainment centers took mini golf to the next level by combining all sorts of activities under one roof.

In addition to mini golf you might find batting cages, video games, pool, and Ping-Pong tables, Skee-Ball, and even bumper cars. Miniature bumper cars, just like the golf! These centers cropped up in the early 1990s while the late nineties revealed yet another twist in the long history of mini golf. Jack Nicklaus's Golden Bear company brought the game to, of all places, the driving ranges. Whether this was to give the kids something to do while Mom and Dad hit a bucket or if it was purely for family fun, who knows? The only thing that matters is the idea caught on and other companies followed suit, pouring millions of dollars into construction. When I lived in Elmsford—thirty minutes north of New York City—The Jimmy and I used to make frequent use of one of Nicklaus's facilities. Just three minutes from our condo, we could hit balls all year round as the range was not only covered but heated as well. The mini golf was a little too serious for my liking—lots of water and no windmills—but the business was booming.

For four years now, ESPN has aired a national miniature golf championship. The world's top sports channel may or may not continue to cover the event, but there's no denying its popularity with the kids. The championships still ranks as one of ESPN's highest rated family programs, right behind "Squash the Violence with Ron Artest" and "Behind the Brim: The Story of Jasper Parnevik's Hats."

If you tear it up on greens both mini and real, you might want to pack that putter up and try your luck against the nation's finest.[38] If you're looking to shed a few pounds, though, I have a better idea . . .

---

[38] *It's probably your best chance of getting on ESPN, too, unless you feel like streaking during a Linda Cohn monologue.*

According to the *Guinness Book of World Records*, up until a few years ago the fastest round of golf ever played was thirty minutes and twenty-two seconds. Upon learning of this record, American runners Dennis Caldwell and Steve Scott—the American record holder for the fastest mile at the time—got together and made some grand plans. Caldwell designed the event and Scott ran it, finishing his round in twenty-nine minutes and thirty seconds. Extreme golf was born.

If you have an instinctive reaction, if your body just jolts into motion upon reading the word "extreme," e-mail this man: bob@competitor.com. Bob will tell you how to set up an extreme golf outing and even an extreme golf league. Like to run? Need to squeeze in your round of golf in less than five hours? Well then, Bob might have what you need.

An editor at *Competitor Magazine*, Bob arranged the first televised extreme golf event back in 1994 and continues to promote the sport today. As evidence of how much this guy likes to do things in a hurry, I e-mailed him for some information and he emailed back within fifteen minutes. Now that's extreme.

Bob's website is *www.extremegolf.com*. The site's slogan is "XTreme Golf . . .Where Speed Is Par for The Course." Bob also likes to call his favorite version of the sport "fitness golf." He writes, "XTreme Golf is looked at in the same way by the purists as snowboarding was."

In a nutshell, you take your score and add it to the time it took, in minutes, to complete the round. Then, subtract your handicap. So let's say you shot a ninety-nine in two hours and ten minutes. Ninety-nine plus 130 is 229. Subtract your twenty-three handicap and the final score (man, forget about running, I'm tired already!) is 206. And a surefire boon to your BMI, as well.

Bob makes a good point when comparing extreme golfers to Olympic biathletes who have to cross-country ski, a tiring anaerobic exercise, and then stop and complete a precise task: shoot at a target. The same can be said of extreme golf, where you need to recover quickly from a sprint to sink a putt. And you'd better hurry up with those shots. In this game, nobody waits. You WILL be hit into if you're lollygagging. And on the green, forget about etiquette. Two golfers may putt at the same time. This process is facilitated by the fact that the pin never leaves the cup.

I, myself, have never played extreme golf. Part of the joy of golf for me is spending a good part of my day in a calm, quiet environment. You see, I'm consistently surrounded by screaming children: my own and my students. So, peace and quiet is a welcome change. Then again, I am getting a bit chubby in my old age. Perhaps sprinting around a golf course would do me some good.[39]

Another golf-in-a-hurry game is Par 3 golf. If regulation golf is Marcia and mini golf is Cindy, well then Par 3 golf is Jan. Actually, Par 3 golf (also called pitch 'n' putt) need not be considered the homely middle sister. When I play, it's on a beautiful little course—ponds, flora, fauna, and all—that's absolutely perfect for working on the short game. And when you're *short* on time, nine holes of two hundred yards or less is just what the doctor/wife ordered.

Most Par 3 courses are also meant to be affordable. Guilford Links was built for residents of this Connecticut town and since I don't live there it costs me a whopping $11 to play. There are so many ways that golf is made available to the average joe, I still can't figure out why the game has such an association with

---

[39] *This from a guy who asks about cart rentals when playing mini golf.*

wealth. Maybe because only wealthy guys can spend enough time playing to actually get better. I know it's what I'd do if I had the time and money!

There are also high-end Par 3-esque golf courses called executive courses, built short and easy so that corporate executives can feel mucho macho—no, no, I jest. They're called executive courses because you are supposed to use executive golf clubs when playing.[40] Still, there does seem to be a socio-economic line of delineation between executive courses and your run-of-the-mill, Cape Cod-type, Par 3 pitch 'n' putts. It's kind of like the difference between a Morton's and an Outback Steakhouse. And I say, gimme the bloomin' onion every time!

In some places, Par 3 golf is referred to as pasture golf (as golf used to be played in pastures). And at *Pasturegolf.com*, I read of a new form of winter golf called "Ten Percent Golf." Although I've only played winter softball, I can see myself letting a well-intentioned buddy talk me into a round. Check it out. The game can be played with any number of people. And the best part is, you don't have to break up into separate groups. It's fun like that Thundering Herd tensome down in Myrtle Beach! The first player hits and his ball becomes the target. Everybody else shoots for it, kind of like in bocce, and the closest player wins. Just so long as s/he is within 10 percent of the target—meaning whatever 10 percent of the initial drive's distance is, marked by paces. If the original shot went sixty yards, the winning shot would have to be within six yards. If nobody gets within six paces, the ball that's farthest away becomes the new target. After that, the rules are up to you and your crazy crew.

---

[40] *These are weird in that they are all woods. I've never seen a set in person, so that's the extent of my knowledge.*

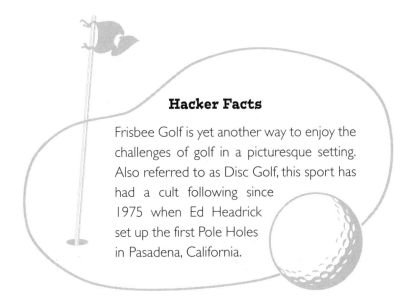

Hacker Facts

Frisbee Golf is yet another way to enjoy the challenges of golf in a picturesque setting. Also referred to as Disc Golf, this sport has had a cult following since 1975 when Ed Headrick set up the first Pole Holes in Pasadena, California.

If you're trying to survive the cold weather months and there's nobody willing to join you on the frozen tundra of a local pasture, well then find yourself an accommodating bar and get a stack of quarters. It's time for Golden Tee.[41]

No way could this book be complete without a mention of Golden Tee. Originally intended to be part of a swing simulator similar to the computer described in the Gear chapter, Golden Tee has emerged as the Pac-Man of the new millennium. Cabbage piqued my interest and next thing I knew, I was reading about Graig Kinzler, the first known professional Golden Tee player in the U.S. While trying to train for Q School—to qualify for the PGA Tour—Kinzler is earning money playing in Golden Tee tournaments.

---

[41] *I'll admit, one reason I love Golden Tee is that this game allows me to feel the joy of scoring birdies while playing golf. Thank you, Golden Tee. Thank you!*

In an article for the *Chicago Tribune*, Whet Moser writes that the game was invented in 1989 and that "it has since become the top-selling arcade game in the country. . . . In the past year, players spent $400 million playing Golden Tee."

Kinzler claims to have earned "about $70,000 last year playing Golden Tee, more than $47,000 in officially sanctioned online tournaments and the rest in live tournaments." And as you can guess by now, "live tournaments" are just ripe for side action.

Kinzler works—I kid you not—with a sports psychologist to hone his Golden Tee skills. He says, "A lot of it is mental. You have to have the confidence that the shot you're hitting is the right shot . . . I've had far more pressure situations to deal with in these Golden Tee tournaments than in real golf." Yeah, but has he had The Jimmy and Ish hazing him? A twelve-pack in his gut with a twelve-foot double Nassau putt on Eighteen? I suppose the answer is yes and then some. Best of luck, Graig!

All of the aforementioned fun: Cabbage with Golden Tee, the orange Fisher-Price putter, and best of all, that MacGilpin sword. Longest Drive, anyone?

Cabbage learned about Golden Tee from his younger brother, Scott. There they go again, those MacGilpin men and their hand-me-down traditions! If you care to speak with them about it after a round chances are you'll find them at The Last Drop in Brighton, Massachusetts. They'll be there to quench their thirst but also to settle the score after eighteen grueling holes. You see, when playing a skins game, there's always the possibility of a carry-over on Eighteen. And how can you settle your bet if the starter won't let you back out for one last hole? Well, you can head to the putting green, as Cabbage and I have done in the past, or you can head to the bar. And it's a bar with Golden Tee, a bar like The Last Drop, that hosts their playoff holes.

The only problem with settling a bet at a bar, Cabbage tells me, is that on more than one occasion neither he nor Scott could remember who came out on top in Golden Tee. As if winning was the point in the first place.

12

Gear II

Three weeks before flying to Mexico for a wedding—and the "Unlimited" golf package at Nuevo Vallarta's Mayan Resort!!!—I decided to have my clubs regripped. As the shopkeep Keith told me, "The grip is the only part of the club you touch." 'Nough said. I was sold.

Everybody from shopkeeps to pros says that you should get your clubs—irons, woods, and wedges—regripped every year or two, but I was never serious enough about the game to sacrifice one greens-fee worth of *dinero* to get new grips. Like I said, though, I'm maturing. I'm learning what it takes to improve.

When I walked in to Golf, Etc., I found a slightly overwhelming display of twenty-plus grips. My options ranged from $2 to $10 per grip and after ten minutes of description and deliberation, I decided on Lamkin Perma-Soft grips. These are supposed to be pretty reliable in that they retain their tackiness, even in inclement weather. They cost $3.50 per club, which seems proportional to the quality of my game (i.e., I ain't no $10 grip of a player!). On their website, Lamkin explains why grips make a difference: "Regripping will not only make your clubs feel new again, new grips will give you the traction and tack you need to make good golf shots. Grips that are worn will slip and increase torque, which means less accurate shot-making."

Upon picking up my new and improved clubs—the turn-around time was one day—I immediately went to the driving range. It was February 3rd and as dreary as dreary gets, but they have heaters over the mats and I had new clubs to try out. Or at least one new club. You see, in addition to the grips, I finally got myself that new 3-wood. Oh baby!!!

Of course I bought more than I intended. That's because, you'll recall, I am an addict. And mark my words, people. I do not regret my purchases. Not one bit. At the driving range it was sheer joy, like the first drive I ever hit way back when. This new club was made for me and I'm just so happy I finally decided to say, "Bye-bye, Big Bertha. Helloooooo, Big Ben!"

The club is a Ben Hogan "Big Ben" c455 Fairway Wood. For the first time, I am hitting a 3-wood with a graphite shaft; its "regular flex" gives me increased whipping action—*fustigaba*, in Spanish—as the club comes around to the point of contact.[42] The ball absolutely rockets off of the club face.

I dropped $180 for my Big Ben and feared the reaction when I submitted my Golf, Etc. expense report to the house manager. But Alicia's reaction was like a renewal of our vows, weekend warrior style.

---

[42] My golfing guru, Mr. Nero, and the shopkeep Keith both recommend getting as much flex as possible, so as to help with distance without sacrificing control.

"Well, your other one was broken right? You *had* to get a new 3-wood." I double-checked for sarcasm and when I detected none, I got up and hugged her. Then I went out to the garage and hugged my new 3-wood.

Upon completion of the book, I brought Big Ben to Mexico for a romantic get-away. Alicia came along, too.

Closing: The Nineteenth Hole

Our food has been ordered, the scores tallied, and the bets settled. The Thundering Herd is gathered in one place for the first time in almost a year and there is no shortage of banter or beer. This is the beauty of the nineteenth hole.

Pulling the old scorecard I'd found in my bag that day out of my pocket, I begin to tell the tale of Johnny Mac's greatest golf moment. Although he played Scotland's Waterville course with his father, I know that his fondest memory came the day before his wedding. It was at Bedford Golf and Tennis's thirteenth, a par-5 516-yard funnel-tight hole.

"It remains the only eagle I've ever seen." I hand him the scorecard and then proceed to relive the moment in real time. "Standing just off the fairway in the second cut, Johnny Mac pulls out a 6-iron. He's looking to bump and run, right up between the two traps guarding the green. All the guy is trying to do is stay straight so he doesn't have to chip over a trap with his next shot."

"F'ing traps," Ish moans. He spent far too much time in the beach today.

I switch into the exaggerated whisper of the golf announcer, a tribute to the game's greats: Nantz and Feherty, McCord and Miller. A little Mike Tirico and Jimmy Roberts, too. "The flag is lifting gently in the September breeze . . . Johnny Mac is seventy yards away. An abbreviated backswing and here we go, folks. This chip looks like a gem."

Most good golf shots introduce themselves right off the club. I don't know how Johnny Mac felt, but the rest of us sensed greatness from the get-go. Our own balls were forgotten as a force greater than Mother Nature, greater than the *Sports Illustrated* swimsuit issue, greater than a two-for-one happy hour drew us towards the green. Slowly at first, then faster, then faster still.

"Forty yards away from pay dirt, the ball touches down and it's right on line. Look at her go. A finely skipped stone riding the surf between those two beaches. A little hot, but hey now! It's hit the lip at the front of that lucky thirteenth green. Johnny Mac is quickly making his way up the fairway as his ball lands on this slightly uphill green with fifteen yards to go. Breaking, it's breaking right to left. This ball is headed for the hole, folks!"

"Even a blind squirrel," The Ice Man deadpans, "finds a nut." But John is enjoying this too much to bother with a reply. Everyone has a moment of greatness, a shot that makes the pros seem not so different, and this is his. On par with the following day's nuptials, I'm sure!

"I get up to the green just in time to see Juan's ball bend left and I can tell it's following a predestined traaaaail to glory," I continue. "Ping then plop, it hits the pin then falls into the hole. You should've seen Johnny Mac trying to hold back that smile. He was the groom and it was *his* day.

"A drive to the fairway, a 5-iron to the rough, and then that chip with his 6—in in three." For the grand finale, I break into song. "I want to fly like an eagle, to the sea. Fly like an eagle, let my 6-iron carry me!"

Someday, one of us will have a story like the four Ernie's friends got to tell. But until that hole-in-one comes along, we'll have to settle for eagles instead of aces.

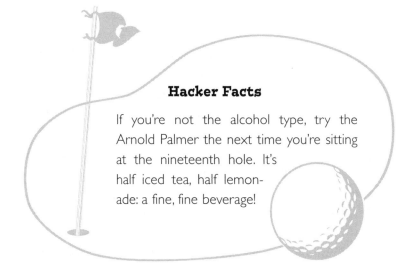

Hacker Facts

If you're not the alcohol type, try the Arnold Palmer the next time you're sitting at the nineteenth hole. It's half iced tea, half lemonade: a fine, fine beverage!

The food arrives and there's a twenty second lull before talk turns to the disappointing Ryder Cup of 2004, the Europeans handing the Americans their hats as we watched from the Murray Brothers' Caddyshack bar on our final day in Myrtle. There's a lot of head shaking and some of the prerequisite theorizing, but just when the cynicism threatens to spoil the mood, ButtNut offers up a fonder memory from the boob tube.

"It's better to remember that sudden death playoff at the 2003 President's Cup, anyway.[43] Great stuff with Tiger and Ernie Els battling it out," he says. "It's unbelievable how well they played under all that pressure. It's tough enough to play for yourself, let alone your country. Both of them made the shots they needed to make. Unlike the Americans at Ryder—"

---

[43] *The President's Cup pits a team from the U.S. against an international squad from countries outside of Europe and is held in non-Ryder Cup years.*

"Unlike us today." We nod in humble agreement. When The Captain speaks, men listen.

"I remember they both parred the first three playoff holes before the match had to be called due to darkness," ButtNut continues. "Imagine in this day and age a sporting event called a tie."

"How'd they decide it?" Cabbage asks, thoughts of Golden Tee on his mind.

"The two sides are splitting time, sharing the Cup one year here, one year there, till they do it again next year, down in Virginia."

The notion of a peaceful accord goes hand-in-hand with the fact that all cell phones have been blessedly silent throughout. The only noise now is the sound of the waitress bringing another round. This is our cue: it's time to revisit that age-old topic, The Jimmy's putting.

"Enough, enough, enough," he waves us off. "I'm happy with my putting."

"I think it could be better." Apparently, ButtNut is done being the ambassador of good will!

"How much *did* that putter run you?" The Holgerdude prods.

"I've told all you bozos a thousand times, it was a present."

We all know this is true, but we also know that the only thing more satisfying than winning Longest Drive is getting a rise out of a friend.

Egg Head, he of golfing gear fame, intones, "I hear that a Scotty Cameron can run a couple hundred bucks. . . ."

"Money," Dr. Dave digs, "you wasted, apparently!"

By now, even The Jimmy is laughing. There's something comforting about traditions, even when they come at your expense.

"Hey," The Ice Man points out, "putts or no putts, he *did* shoot an 84 today."

Tuppa keeps the spotlight on The Jimmy, but in a more constructive way, asking him about his date with Amy Mickelson. As

Phil is the god of our golfing world, she is the goddess. The Mickelsons: the first family of golf.

"It was at the 1999 Ryder Cup at Brookline. During the big U.S. comeback," The Jimmy beams, "Amy walked by and gave me a high-five. I think we were on the sixteenth or seventeenth. Next thing, you know, everyone's hugging on the green and spraying champagne from the balcony!"

No nineteenth hole is complete without a golf story of this kind. It's a way to wed professional golf and our hacker's game; a way to make us all feel a little better about the scorecards laying face down on the table. Today, we benefit from two tales as Phat Head goes beyond Amy and straight to Phil.

"I was working as a grip at the 1998 MCI Classic in Harbour Town. It was the third round and we were assigned to Phil."

"It's a cruel world," Johnny Mac sighs, "when a man has to work under such conditions."

"Worked my fingers to the bone and didn't enjoy for one minute all that fly-on-the-wall, front-row exposure to great golf shots and the banter between him and his caddy, Jim 'Bones' MacKay. Seriously, both of them are salt of the earth. Genuinely nice guys. They even gave me the head-nod that night at a great Mexican restaurant called Aunt Chiladas. Is it fringe benefits or French benefits?"

"You are a jackass," which, of course is Man Code for "I'd drive three hours for a round of golf with you."

Phat Head acknowledges this with a smile—wouldn't you be grinning if you'd just shot an 82?—then polishes off the last of the Coors Lite. Ten-dollar bills fall to the table like well-placed approach shots and that's that. Chairs pushed back from the table and handshakes all around. It's the end of another outing, old memories recalled and a few more memories made. Nobody can wait for the next nineteen. Not a one of us.

My Babblography

Forget having a bibliography. Nobody ever reads 'em, anyway! I'm going to do you a favor, instead. Many a good book has been recommended to me while tripping the course fantastic, so I'm going to do the same for you.

Here, in alphabetical order, are some writers and books that I highly recommend: *Classic Golf Tips* by Tommy Armour; David Feherty; anything, golf and otherwise, by John Feinstein; David Leadbetter; *Cinderella Story* by Bill Murray; Dave Pelz; *Harvey Penick's Little Red Book*; *Chi Chi's Golf Games You Gotta Play*, by Chi Chi Rodriguez; and Dr. Gary Wiren. But there is one writer I'd like to spend a little extra time on in this here babblography and his name is P. G. Wodehouse.

For every ball you find in a large bucket of range balls, there's a Wodehouse story about golf. Read and you'll find men driven to the point of personal and financial ruin—and sometimes both—by this beloved game of ours. And always in a humorous manner.

One memorable Wodehousian golfer was Mitchell Holmes, a man who blames the "uproar of butterflies in the adjoining meadow" whenever he misses a putt. Then there is Rollo Podmarch who is very good at golf . . . according to his mother. She brags because her boy Rollo manages to score more than 120 every time out! Even better is Wodehouse's most memorable golfing creation, the Eldest Member. This wise old sage perches on the terrace outside the Marvis Bay Golf and Country Club, observing the comings and goings of all the club's members. He describes the Eldest Member as follows: "The eye of the Eldest

Member was thoughtful and reflective. When it looked into yours you saw in it that perfect peace, that peace beyond understanding, which comes at its maximum only to the man who has given up golf."

That's a peace I'd rather live without. You and me and our man, P. G.